HOW TO FIND A BARGAIN HOME

by

ROBERT HANCOCK

AND

ELIZABETH ASHTON

BROUGHTON HALL, INC.
Eighth Edition
Copyright ©1993

ISBN 0-934748-22-5

Manufactured in the United States of America

PUBLISHER'S NOTE

We have done our best to carefully research and compile this Directory only from sources believed to be authentic and reliable; however, we cannot guarantee total accuracy or completeness.

If you would be kind enough to bring to our attention any errors you may find, we will include your corrections in our next edition. We will also send you a complimentary copy of one of our other books as a token of our appreciation.

Please note we are publishers and are not affiliated with any governmental agency. However, the material used in this Directory is drawn in part from government publications, and their contribution is gratefully acknowledged. Our sole purpose is to provide you with a fund of useful information that will help you find a bargain home.

Good luck in your house buying.

THE PUBLISHERS

TABLE OF CONTENTS

1.0 FOREWORD

Thank you for purchasing this directory. Our research team has spent hundreds of hours gathering a wealth of information that will help you realize one of the most exciting of all achievements: owning your own home or developing investment property.

We want you to use this directory like a handbook: peruse the dozens of different government programs we describe, and follow our instructions for the ones that suit you best. Once you're familiar with the information presented here, you will be able to ask the right questions in the right places of the right people, and you will get the help you need to buy the home you want at a price you can afford.

I'm not going to pretend it doesn't require a lot of effort and determination. If you thumb through the book, make one or two phone calls, then say, "I'm not going to go through all that to get a home!" — well, either you can afford to buy a home through the usual channels, or you simply don't want your own home very much.

I'm talking to those of you who cannot afford a home without some assistance: YOU ARE THE PEOPLE FOR WHOM THESE GOVERNMENT SUBSIDY PROGRAMS WERE DESIGNED. There are people who want to help you, but they cannot do it for you; you are responsible for helping yourself to these government programs.

The important thing now is to USE this information. Only if you do will it be worth many times the money you have paid for it. Remember, it is a working manual: make notations in the pages as you go along and in the margins as you work with it.

You've been smart enough to invest in this Directory — now make it the BEST investment you've ever made. No matter how tight the housing market, don't let anyone tell you that you cannot find bargain priced homes. There are many ways to do it. Start reading right now to find the way that's best for YOU.

2.0   <u>INTRODUCTION</u>

Did you know that Uncle Sam would like nothing better than to see you living in a safe, decent home of your own, making reasonable payments? Pretty surprising news, isn't it? Especially when you read in the paper every day about how fewer and fewer people in the United States can afford to purchase homes.

Well, the Federal Government reads the paper, too. In fact, the Federal Government has a lot more information at its disposal than just what they read in the papers. And believe it or not, they are concerned about the problem. When the housing prices started really soaring in the late 1970's, a number of programs were introduced at all levels of government to assist moderate income families to purchase a home of their own.

In the government's eyes, a family with an average income should be able to buy an average home. But you know that this is no longer true today. We've all heard tales about two income *couples* who can't even afford to buy a home. The Federal Government does not feel people should have to pay more than 1/3 of their monthly income toward housing. By 1979, the interest rates and mortgage terms were so steep that most people were priced out of the housing market. Today, only about 15% of first-time homebuyers can afford to buy an average new home and 60% of the people living in homes already would not be able to buy them at today's prices.

You might ask, "Why should the Federal Government care if I can't afford to buy a home?" Well, there are a lot of reasons: It is not healthy for the community to have a high percentage of renters — they have little incentive to keep up the property and they are not usually interested in the community, *per se*, as a homeowner would be. Also, a largely rental community is less stable than a community of largely homeowners. When people have to pay a high proportion of their income toward their housing, they have little left to spend on education, vacations, home improvement and disposable income type purchases. This situation leads to problems. People who cannot afford adequate housing will tend to crowd too many people into one house, and that breeds many problems and unhappiness. When prices are too high, even people who currently own homes are affected because they don't have the freedom to move, since moving to even a smaller home would probably cost them more than staying where they are. Thousands of jobs depend on a healthy building industry, manufacturing, transportation, furnishings and so forth. Overpriced housing deadens a large segment of our economy.

A dead economy does our government no good at all. The government has done studies which show that a typical $70,000 house will generate about $1,260 a year in local property taxes. Other benefits pile up from that starting point — more jobs are available, people stay in the community longer, they get involved in the community and try to correct any problems that might exist, and the entire economy grows and prospers.

When I first got wind of these government-subsidized programs that are available, I could hardly believe my eyes as I read them: 3% down, 3% interest on mortgage loans, *homes given away* for people to rehabilitate with a low interest loan, interest rates adjusted so that you won't be paying more than 1/3 of your monthly income toward your house payment... "These are just too good to be true," I said to myself, "there has to be a catch!" Well, there is a catch, and it is the same catch that all government programs have, and that is: *YOU HAVE TO KNOW ABOUT THE PROGRAMS BEFORE YOU CAN ASK FOR THEM.* Now that doesn't sound very difficult, but it is a very big hurdle. The government has all these wonderful, generous programs to help us, but there are so many, and each program has different requirements and regulations and is administered by a different person or a different office — it can make you give up in frustration very quickly.

I found myself calling Los Angeles time after time to inquire about the programs generally, and you cannot get away with that: they have to know *exactly* what you want information about, since each government employee seems to know only about his particular department. In fact, the HUD office in Los Angeles is famous for its busy telephone. I called for two weeks before I finally got a ring, then it rang for almost an hour (seriously!) before it was answered. The important thing to remember is, *this is not done purposely to irritate you or to make it difficult for you to find out the information*. The reason is simply that these people are extremely busy and understaffed and they can only do so much. Obviously, a lot of people are going to give up at this stage, before they have even found out the first thing about the loans available. Please promise me you won't give up. You know why? Because to your great surprise and pleasure, you will find the government employees are not only pleasant and helpful, but they **want** to help you get an affordable home. That is the whole purpose of their job.

There has been some talk in the newspapers about the possibility of the Federal Government cutting some housing funds about 10%. Well, even if they did, there are still going to be plenty of funds there. For example, an article from our local Santa Barbara paper mentioned the possibility of these fund cuts — there will still be around $1,000,000 to use! Someone is going to get to use that $1,000,000 — why shouldn't that someone by <u>YOU</u>? (We're referring to similar programs in your own town, of course). Are you going to let someone else have the house YOU could have had if only you would have made one more phone call, if only you would have awakened a little earlier and been waiting in line before the next guy?

Those fund cuts are only from the federal level — there are MANY, MANY programs at state, county and government levels which are *in addition* to the federal programs. You should always start at your most local level: *the city housing office*, and find out which programs are active in your particular area. A good idea is to contact a real estate agent and ask what rehab loans, which mortgages, which development funds are available in your area. They are in the business of knowing what is going on in the housing market. You may not find the information you need from the first agent you talk to, but keep making phone calls and asking questions until you find the person able and willing to help you. Just as it is with government employees, not every individual will know about every program, but keep asking and you will find the person who has the information you need.

Get to know the nice people in the city, county and state housing offices. They are not faceless "civil servants," but individuals just like you and me. If you are polite and show them you are truly interested in finding a home for your family and that you want to be cooperative, they will help you as much as they can. You may have to go from one to the next, to the next and again to the next, BUT YOU WILL GET THERE. THERE IS A PROGRAM FOR YOU — YOU JUST HAVE TO STICK WITH IT UNTIL YOU FIND IT.

You know, the United States has a lot of self-made millionaires, and they did not get where they are by expecting other people to do everything for them. No. They know the best job is one they do themselves. They control their life. They get in there and work hard. That way, they know what they are doing and they have confidence. Then when they succeed, they have themselves to thank and they also have the knowledge that they could do it again if they had to. So think of this getting a bargain home as a way of developing your knowledge and your self-confidence as well as your financial stability.

So, now you know that the government wants you to have your own home (and that means all levels of government, from federal all the way down to city) and the government employees want to help you utilize the programs they are in charge of. The only thing left is to read about what programs are available and to get started!

3.0   HOW DO I START?

STEPS TO TAKE IN FINDING GOVERNMENT HELP

Sometimes it's difficult to know exactly what kind of questions to ask and exactly which agencies to call when you're looking for the information that will lead you to that bargain home. Each city, county and/or state can have its own programs and procedures for getting on the programs, so you need to know how to get this information. You must also know exactly what it is you are looking for. Do you want to buy a single family home? Would you like to buy a whole set of apartments and rent to low-income people and have the government subsidize the rents to you? Or would you prefer to live in a brand new home or condo? Are you a first-time or low-income homebuyer? An investor? Once you know what you want, you can confidently request information for your specific situation.

We've listed here some of the questions WE ask when we want to find out about programs in your area, so we know these questions get results. Try them for yourself and see.

Before you start making calls, however, you should read this directory thoroughly so you'll know *which programs* you are most interested in and will better understand the information given to you by various agencies and lending institutions.

NOTE: Many of our readers have been calling HUD to ask about "their loans"; please realize *HUD is not a lending institution and DOES NOT make loans.* Some of HUD's functions are to guarantee or insure loans which you receive through regular lenders. (HUD *may* be able to tell you which lenders are approved by them, but your best bet is to call lenders on your own and get the best rates. Ask, when you call each one, whether they are a HUD-approved lender; if they are, ask what their rates are for the amount you want to borrow under the program you are interested in.)

Never sit down to make calls without having a pen and notebook handy to write down the information you get. Three or four calls may get you so much information you won't remember which office told you what. To help you keep everything straight, we've made up a worksheet (see Appendix 2, page 161) which you may find useful.

FIRST look in the front of your phone book under City and County governments and locate the numbers for Department of Housing, Community Redevelopment, Community Rehabilitation, or any other department which refers to housing of any kind. Write ALL numbers down. If you cannot find the numbers, call information and ask the operator if he or she can help you find numbers for those or similar agencies. Tell the operator you'd like as many numbers as you can get.

NEXT call *each and every department* you have a number for and ask:

Do you have any loans available for first-time (or low-income, if applicable) homebuyers?

If you get a "yes" answer, ask the person to explain what types of programs they have. After getting the information from them, say:

Thank you. Do you know of any other agencies I can call for additional housing program information?

You just may end up with more numbers than you had to begin with, and a LOT of great information!

If you get a "no" answer, ask:

What kinds of programs do you operate with your funds?

Chances are they may have something of interest to you, such as rehabilitation loans or grants. Again, *ask them* if they have any suggestions for you regarding *who to call for additional information.*

Now ask the agency:

Do you know of any HUD-approved counselors for PRE-purchase counseling?

There aren't many of these around, but if you can find one, counseling can help you become aware of — and take advantage of — the many programs which are somewhat elusive to the casual observer.

You will probably be asked by the agencies you call for personal information which will aid them in finding a program to help you. The type of information they will be looking for is this: How many in the the household; total household income ("**low income" can be quite liberal;** ask what the limitations are, and *remember*, **limits are not always the same in every agency or for every program**); whether you have any savings and/or can afford a small down payment; whether the purchaser(s) is elderly, disabled, a widow/widower or single parent with several dependents; whether the purchaser is a veteran, handicapped, etc. They want factual information on your personal situation, so you may want to write down everything you think would help to qualify you for assistance in obtaining a home.

Before calling a LENDER (which can be a bank or a real estate finance company), you should know exactly which program(s) you are interested in. Ask to speak with a loan officer, then ask:

Do you currently work with HUD-insured loans?

If they do, ask if they are familiar with the type of loan you are looking for. If they are, get their rates, then call another lender, then another — get *all* the rates you can; some will be better than others.

See, you have to dig. There is no way anyone can tell you exactly where to go and exactly what to ask for, but spending some of your time seeking out the government's fabulous programs is really worthwhile. It probably means the difference between you buying a home or not being able to!

One last note before you get started. Remember when you call government agencies that *each agency you talk to is probably only going to be aware of and familiar with ITS OWN PROGRAM*. If a person tells you "I have no idea what you're talking about," it doesn't mean the program doesn't exist, it means **that** person in **that** agency doesn't know about the program. So don't stop at one agency or even one person at each agency. Ask (politely!) if there is anyone else there who might be able to help you, and ask each agency if they would recommend that you call anyone else for more information. Many times agencies won't volunteer information, but they will answer your questions truthfully. So ask, **ask, ASK!**

4.0   <u>THE FOUR TYPES OF GOVERNMENT LOANS</u>

There are four basic types of real estate loans authorized by Congress to be made by primary lenders to the real estate consumer in the U.S. The following is a brief summary of these loan types:

(1)   *INSURED LOANS*: An insured loan is underwritten and funded by a primary lender and is insured by a governmental entity. The U.S. Department of Housing and Urban Development (HUD) is currently the only governmental entity that issues insurance policies on real estate loans made by primary lenders.

Under a government insured real estate loan, the lender who makes the loan to the consumer is insured by the government against possible loss of money due to a buyer defaulting (not making timely payments) which may or may not result in a foreclosure action. When an individual enters into an agreement with a primary lender to accept a government insured loan, that individual becomes responsible for paying an insurance premium to the government. The insurance premium is called a Mortgage Insurance Premium (MIP). Under the MIP system, the individual seeking an insured loan is expected to pay the entire insurance premium on the date they receive the real estate loan.

Since one advantage of an insured loan is a low down payment structure, the total MIP premium is added to the loan balance and this entire fee is forwarded immediately to the Distributive Share Section of HUD upon the close of the loan. Under this payment structure, if your loan balance was $35,000 at the time of closing and your MIP premium was an additional $800.00, your home loan balance would be increased to $35,800.00 and appropriate interest would be charged by the lender for the additional balance.

Until 1976, the Distributive Share Section placed premiums for MIP into a distributive pool fund. The Distributive Share Section was negligent in informing the consumer who eventually paid off his or her loan that he or she was entitled to a partial refund. HUD and the Distributive Share Section were charged with negligence in disbursing these refunds to the consumer. If you (or someone you know) has ever had a government insured loan that you have paid off, you may be due a refund. You can find out by calling (202) 755-5616 to obtain the forms necessary for filing a claim.

There are some drawbacks to a government insured loan. The most obvious is the Government's right of eminent domain. The United States Government is the sovereign power of the land, so if you accept a government insured loan from a primary lender and default on the loan for any reason, the Federal Government is authorized by Congress to seek reimbursement for any loss created. In other words, if you obtain a government insured loan for fifty thousand dollars and default, when a foreclosure sale takes place—if your property sells for anything less than the fifty thousand dollars (plus accrued interest and foreclosure costs—the government can seek and receive a deficiency judgment against you. If you are unable to pay the accrued costs at the time of the judgment, the government may file a lien against you (which can reflect on your credit report).

An important advantage to a government insured loan is the "buyer to assume the loan balance" assumption clause in the mortgage. When the original owner sells his/her property to another under this clause, the new buyer pays a fee equal to one percent of the existing loan balance at the time of the close of escrow. This clause also requires the new buyer to qualify for the loan. If the new buyer assumes the loan under these conditions, the new buyer becomes totally responsible for the loan and, if a default occurs in the future, the original buyer cannot be held responsible for any deficiency judgment.

(2)   *GUARANTEED LOANS*: A guaranteed loan is similar to an insured loan with one major difference — an insured loan protects primary lenders against default by issuing an insured policy which clearly states a *percentage* which the primary lender can receive, and a guaranteed loan states a *specific dollar amount* that can be received by the primary lender if default occurs in the future, once the loan is made.

The U.S. Department of Housing and Urban Development (HUD) presently makes only one type of guaranteed loan, which is for multifamily apartments designed for the elderly and handicapped, and all of the newly created U.S. Department of Veteran Affairs loans fall into the guaranteed status. Loans given by the U.S. Department of Agriculture and the Small Business Administration also fall into the category of guaranteed loans.

Guaranteed loans also contain the "subject to loan balance" and "buyer to assume loan balance" clauses. When a veteran uses his/her benefits to acquire property and then sells it to another person, unless the new buyer is also a qualified veteran and the seller completes and files a "Release of Liability" form with the local U.S. Department of Veteran Affairs Office prior to the loan's close, the original veteran may be subject to a deficiency judgment.

(3)   *DIRECT LOANS*: A direct loan is one whereby you go directly to the government agency and apply for a loan that is funded by that governmental agency. Direct loans at the federal level are disbursed by the U.S. Department of Agriculture, Farmers Home Administration. At the state, county, or city level, the funds are disbursed by a recognized political subdivision of our government.

Direct loans have two advantages: first, the consumer doesn't have to go through a middle man (i.e. bank, savings and loan, or mortgage banker) to apply. Rather, the application goes directly to a governmental agency, and the approval or rejection of the loan is made locally; the second advantage to a direct loan is that since there is no middle man, the interest rate charged to the consumer is less.

(4)   *BONDED LOANS*: The Industrial Development Bond Act (IRS Code 103(b)) allows for private investors to invest money in corporate expansion. Interest gained from these transactions is tax free. This Code also gave authority to state, county and city level governments tot form their own "bonding agency" if they meet certain financial obligations.

Under the Industrial Development Bond Act (IDBA), newly created corporations or existing corporations can receive capital infusions to expand their operations. In order to receive an Industrial Development Bond, the expanding corporation must show necessity for the capital requested and a business plan which will hire ten or more new employees. Additionally, the capital must be used to either build a new facility or rehabilitate an existing facility or plant.

5.0   FINDING A GOOD PLACE TO LIVE

One of the first "rules of thumb" you'll want to keep in mind when you begin looking for a home is that whether you are buying your first home or your umpteenth, you should be treating the purchase as an investment. While owning a home is part of the American Dream, it is important that you keep your emotions at bay and look at each property not only as a place to live, but as a means of investing in your future.

More millionaires make their fortunes in real estate then in the stock market — so just because you are currently looking for a bargain, don't forget that today's bargain may be tomorrow's bankroll!

Since purchasing your home(s) may be the single largest investment in your life, it is important that you shop wisely. Even in lean times, real estate tends to appreciate, and if you purchase a property that has potential (i.e. room for additions, improvements, etc.) you are bound to come out ahead.

Let's take a look at some of the things you should be considering when shopping for a home.

One of your first concerns will be the community. When you settle in a particular area you become involved with the day-to-day plans and problems. Pride in ownership should give you a sense of responsibility and the desire to have a voice in policies which your community makes.

If you are a "city slicker" you'll choose your community for the shopping areas, availability of creature comforts like theaters, restaurants and health clubs, transportation, etc.

On the other hand, if you prefer a quieter life, you may wish to live in the suburbs, where you may have to contend with somewhat limited transportation, fewer shopping opportunities, schools, and so on.

Some of you may even opt for country living, which provides its own set of pros and cons. Regardless of your choice, you'll want to make sure that you have weighed all of the possibilities before you reach a decision to purchase a home in a particular location.

5.1   Deciding if You're Ready to Buy

There are several factors to consider prior to buying a house. To make a realistic choice you must decide how much you can afford to spend on the property.

Are you going to live in the home for several years? In the early life of a mortgage, the bulk of your payment goes to interest, so you are acquiring very little in the way of equity. The longer you hold on to a property, the more equity you will acquire.

Another consideration is your ability to meet house payments. If you are buying a house according to the conventional method, a good guideline would be that the price of your home should not exceed two times your annual family income. Additionally, you should not pay more than 38% of family income after federal tax for monthly housing expense (payment on the mortgage loan plus average cost of heat, utilities, repair and maintenance).

You should have the cash necessary to meet the down payment and other closing expenses. You will need to find a realtor you can trust and depend upon, and then have this person (or the lender) provide an estimate of all closing costs you will need. Congress passed the Real Estate Settlement Procedures Act (RESPA) to protect homebuyers from unnecessarily high settlement costs. It requires advance estimates of settlement costs, limits the size of escrow accounts and prohibits referral fees and kickbacks.

RESPA requires that all borrowers of federally related mortgage loans receive from the lender a HUD prepared booklet containing information about real estate transactions, settlement services, cost comparisons and relevant consumer protection laws when applying for a loan.

If you desire further information on how RESPA is watching out for your rights when purchasing a home, you can send your inquiry to:

U.S. Department of Housing and Urban Development
Office of Single Family Housing
451 7th Street South West
Washington, D.C. 20410

5.2   How to Find the Right House for You

There are numerous ways to shop for the house that is just right for you and your family. Some of the obvious include:

(1)   Read the advertisements in the real estate section of your local newspaper.

(2)   Let your friends, neighbors and business associates know that you are house hunting. Networking is very valuable when dealing with real estate! Don't stop looking until you have a clear idea of the cost and quality of homes presently being offered for sale.

(3)   Take a weekend afternoon and drive or walk through neighborhoods you find desirable. You may come upon an unadvertised "gem," or meet someone who knows of a home for sale that fits your needs.

(4)   Keep a record of homes that interest you, including the asking price, the owner's name, location, number of bedrooms, taxes, utility bills, and any special features.

5.3   Do You Want a New or Used House?

Two out of every three home buyers select a used house. The one person out of three who buys a new house usually purchases one that is already built rather than building his/her own. Choosing new or used is something you will have to weigh for yourself. Generally speaking, an older home has the advantage of offering you more house for the money. Older homes usually have existing landscaping, so you don't have the added expense of planting trees and shrubs. Taxes are usually stable in an established neighborhood. Even the time it takes to commute is generally shorter from older, more established neighborhoods.

Prior to investing in older neighborhoods, you'll want to check on any future plans for neighborhood improvements, urban renewal or land appropriations for new highways or other projects.

Once you've found a house you like, evaluate it carefully. You are buying the property "as is" and this is one instance where you literally will have to *live* with any mistakes you make!

5.4   When You Decide to Buy an Older Home

What at first appears to be a bargain home may turn into a real headache if you don't make a thorough inspection prior to your decision. Obviously, if you are contemplating a homesteading property, you will be expecting flaws that are fixable. However, if you are buying through more conventional means, you will want to check the construction of the house for soundness. Older homes need special attention in the following area — make sure you take this checklist with you when you are shopping!

(1)   TERMITE INFESTATION AND WOOD ROT. Having a termite specialist check the property is a must. You will be wise if you include a termite clause in any contract you consider which gives certification of termite inspection and guarantee.

(2)   STRUCTURAL FAILURE. Make sure that you examine for a sagging roof, cracked walls or slabs, uneven floors or other evidence of supporting soil or poor bearing capacity, or inadequate structural members or fastenings.

(3)   INADEQUATE WIRING. Be sure that there is sufficient amperage and enough electrical outlets. You should request an inspection by the local building inspector for code compliance to make sure the wiring is in good shape.

(4)   A RUN DOWN FURNACE. Check the general condition of the heating system. Many older homes have

steam heat systems that are on their last legs — have someone check out the system in the home you are contemplating, and if work will be needed, be sure you find out if parts are even available for your older system or if a whole new unit will be necessary. In a large older home, putting in a new heating (and/or cooling system) will run you several thousand dollars. You'll want to know if this is an expense that will be necessary prior to signing on the dotted line. Remember, oftentimes if you find out about things that need to be repaired prior to making your deal, you can either have the owner take care of these things prior to sale, or work out a deal whereby the price is reduced to allow for the necessary repairs.

(5)   INADEQUATE INSULATION. Find out if the attic and the space between interior and exterior walls has been filled with an insulating material. You'll also want to know what material was used and how it was installed. Many older homes do not have adequate insulation, which can greatly affect your heating and cooling bills. A home isn't much of a bargain if you are only paying a house payment of $200 or $300 each month, and have utility bills that closely approach or surpass that figure!

(6)   FAULTY PLUMBING. If possible, choose a home that is connected to a public sewer system rather than served by a septic tank or cesspool. Check with the plumber who first serviced the house to find out its condition, and ask him to check the water pressure for you.

(7)   HOT WATER HEATER. Make sure you know the type and capacity of the tank so that you will know if there will be sufficient hot water for your family's needs. Look for any signs of rust or leaks. If there is a guarantee that still applies, make sure you get a copy.

(8)   ROOF AND GUTTERS. What kind of roofing material was used and how old is it? Check inside the attic for

water stains and discolorations. Talk to the owner about any guarantee that may still exist on the roof.

(9)   WET BASEMENTS. Signs of water in a basement can indicate that the entire structure of your home may be in jeopardy. Take a look at the foundation walls to see if there are any signs of water penetration. If there is a dehumidifier in the basement, you may want to ask some questions! There is nothing wrong with damp air in a basement, but if springtime brings four inches of water, you'll want to know!

(10)   OVERALL CONSIDERATIONS. Examine the conditions of the outside paint and the paint and wall-paper inside the house. Make certain that all the windows and doors operate and are in good repair. If there is a fireplace, it should have a workable damper. Inspect floor and wall tile and fixtures in the bathroom. Make sure the attic has sufficient storage areas.

Bear in mind that there is no perfect house. You just want to be aware, in advance, of the shortcomings of the house you are buying.

5.5   When Buying a New House

Once you have weighed all of the factors and you decide that a new home will best meet your needs, you will want to keep the following in mind:

(1)   The reliability of the builder is a critical consideration in choosing a new home. A reputable builder is in business for life. Arrange to talk with people who are living in houses constructed by the builder you are considering.

(2)   Don't be overwhelmed by the appearance of a glittering model home. Make sure you know exactly what features are provided with your new house, and which are "extras" that are on display in the model.

(3)   Be sure the contract is complete and that there is agreement on all the details of the transaction. Don't

make assumptions about what features are included in the contract and later find out you've misunderstood.

(4)   If the community is to have new street paving, water, sewer lines and sidewalks, make sure you know about local charges for water and trash collection.

(5)   Take a look at the lot site in advance. Is it the size and setting you want for your house?

(6)   Make sure that you personally know about the zoning uses permitted for the area in which you are planning to buy a home. Find out if the neighborhood is strictly residential or zoned for commercial uses. This information could affect your future property value. The city, county, or township clerk's office can tell you where you need to inquire about zoning.

(7)   Your contract with the builder should set forth the total sales price. Whenever possible, you should find a lender who will allow you to take advantage of lower interest rates which may apply at the time of closing. In any event, avoid an arrangement which would allow the lender to increase the mortgage interest rate if market conditions change between the date of the mortgage commitment and the closing date of your new home.

(9)   Check on the progress of the construction on a regular basis, so that you aren't thrown any surprises.

(10) If there are extra features that you want included in the furnished house, make sure that you have the details in writing.

(11) Prior to taking title to the house, make a thorough inspection trip. Check all equipment, windows, and doors. This will be your last chance to request changes.

(12) When you take possession, you must *insist* that you have in your possession the following:

     (a)   warranties from all manufacturers for equipment in the house,

     (b)   certificate of occupancy, and

     (c)   certificates from the Health Department clearing plumbing and sewer installations.

You will also be wise to obtain all applicable certificates of code compliance.

6.0   URBAN HOMESTEADING PROGRAMS

6.1   New Programs Available

Urban Homesteading began as a national program to revitalize declining neighborhoods and reduce the inventory of federally-owned properties by transferring vacant and unrepaired single-family properties to new homeowners for repair and rehabilitation. Properties that are owned by HUD, the Veterans Administration (VA) and Farmers Home Administration (FMHA) may be used in this program.

The Urban Homesteading program was highly successful in many cities across the United States for 15 years. This program has, however, been phased out on a national level since 1990. Urban Homesteading programs may still be in effect in your area, but they are no longer tied in with the Federal government, and are now run strictly at a local level. Does this mean you won't be able to find affordable housing in your area? *ABSOLUTELY NOT!* The government has implemented two new programs aimed at low-income families, renters and first-time home buyers, which will fill the gaps left by the demise of Urban Homesteading.

One new program is called **THE HOME PROGRAM**. This program was created under Title II (The Home Investment Partnerships Act) of the National Affordable Housing Act of 1990. Generally, this program is designed:

- To expand the supply of decent and affordable housing, particularly rental housing, for low and very low income Americans. Such housing includes existing rental housing made affordable through tenant-based rental assistance.

- To strengthen the abilities of state and local governments to design and implement strategies for achieving adequate supplies of decent, affordable housing.

24

- To provide both financial and technical assistance to participating jurisdictions, including the development of model programs for affordable low-income housing.

- To extend and strengthen partnerships among all levels of government and the private sector, including for-profit and nonprofit organizations, in the production of operation of affordable housing.

The HOME Program is not a categorical housing program, such as public housing new construction, requiring a specific housing activity. Rather, the HOME Program provides states and local governments flexibility to decide what kind of housing assistance, or mix of housing assistance, is most appropriate to meet their housing needs.

HOME Program funds have already been allocated and are now in place in 400 communities throughout the U.S. You may wish to contact the local agency listed for your area to find out if this program is available where you live. While you are asking questions, it won't hurt for you to find out if there is still any type of Urban Homesteading program available in your area too!

HOME funds may be used for a variety of activities to develop and support affordable housing. Eligible activities include: Tenant-based rental assistance, assistance to first-time homebuyers and existing homeowners, property acquisitions, new construction, reconstruction, moderate or substantial rehabilitation, site improvements, demolition, relocation expenses and other reasonable and necessary expenses related to the development of non-luxury housing.

WHAT WILL ENSURE THAT LOW AND VERY LOW-INCOME FAMILIES ARE SERVED?

Rental Housing — HOME funds invested in rental housing must meet the following income targeting requirements for the program as a whole:

- As least 90 percent of such funds must be invested in units that are occupied by families whose incomes do not exceed 60 percent of the median family income for the area; and

- The remaining funds (up to 10 percent) must be invested in units occupied by families below 80 percent of median income.

Each rental project must also meet the following affordability tests: Rents must be at or below the LESSER of either the existing Section 8 Fair Market Rent, or 30 percent of the adjusted income of a family whose income equals 65 percent of the median income for the area. They must also remain affordable for the following terms on the average HOME subsidy per unit:

Rehabilitation of up to $15,000	5 years
Rehabilitation of $15,000 - $40,000	10 years
Rehabilitation of $40,000+	15 years
New Construction (any amount)	20 years

Lastly, at least 20 percent of its units must be occupied by very low income families paying not more than 30 percent of monthly adjusted gross income for rent, or bearing rents not greater than 30 percent of the gross income of a family whose income equals 50 percent of the median income for the area.

Homeownership — All of the HOME funds used for homeownership assistance must benefit first-time homebuyers (including displaced homemakers and single parents who may have once owned a home with a spouse), or existing low-income homeowners whose family incomes are at or below 80% of the area median income. In addition, the assisted housing must be the owner's principal residence. The purchase price of the property, or the appraised value of a property already owned, after rehabilitation must be less than 95 percent of median area purchase price; and resale of the property by a first-time homebuyer must be restricted to low income homebuyers at a price that will yield a fair return to the seller and be affordable to the new owner.

The second program, **HOPE 3/SINGLE FAMILY HOMEOWNERSHIP**, will be funded in September 1992. This program has been designed to replace the old Urban Homesteading Program, but it will be up to each city to determine how the monies will be allocated. Although this program is not yet in place, you will definitely want to know about it so that when it is implemented you can benefit! Basically, HOPE 3 will assist low income families in becoming homeowners by providing planning and implementation grants to organizations that will help individual families purchase single-family homes (4 units or fewer) owned by the Department of Housing and Urban Development, Department of Veterans Affairs, Department of Agriculture, Resolution Trust Corporation (TRC), state and local governments, or public or Indian housing authorities.

HOPE 3 has outlined the steps from poverty to homeownership to include: Securing, stabilizing and improving the community; implementing resident management; creating jobs and economic opportunities; and designing and executing homeownership plans. The HOPE program has over ONE BILLION DOLLARS to help in its efforts.

So there you have it, a brief overview of the programs which may help you obtain either rental assistance or the ability to become a homeowner. Your best bet right now is to call your local contact office to see which of these programs are available in your area. You may also want to contact your nearest HUD office to obtain literature on these programs. Once the HOPE 3 monies have been allocated in the fall, you will be able to get a list of where the program has been implemented. Finding out about the program early will put you way ahead when it comes to getting a home of your own!

LOCAL AGENCY CONTACTS

Alabama, Birmingham
Mr. Forrest Davis
Urban Homesteading Coordinator
Department of Community
Development & Housing
City Hall, Room 700
710 North 20th Street
Birmingham, AL 35203
(205) 254-2723

Arizona, Phoenix
Ms. Joyce Ewing
Finance Supervisor
Neighborhood Improvement &
Housing Department
920 Madison
Phoenix, AZ 85034
(602) 262-6952

Colorado, Denver
Ms. Olivia Lucero-Thompson
D.U.R.A.
999 18th Street
Denver, CO 80202
(303) 295-3872

Florida, Broward County
Ms. Edna M. Frazier
Housing Programs Coordinator
Broward County, Community
Development Division
P.O. Box 14668
Fort Lauderdale, FL 33301

Florida, Dade County
Ms. Vivian Bryant
Urban Homesteading Coordinator
Community & Economic Dev.
140 West Flagler Street
Miami, FL 33131
(305) 375-3455

Florida, Fort Lauderdale
Mr. Charles Adams
Community Devel. Coordinator
Department of Planning &
Community Development
101 North Andrews Avenue
P.O. Box 14250
Fort Lauderdale, FL 33302
(305) 761-5281

Florida, Hillsborough County
Ms. Paulette Scannell
Rehabilitation Counselor
Community Code Enforcement
County of Hillsborough
P.O. Box 1110
Tampa, FL 33619
(813) 623-2881

Florida, Jacksonville
Mr. Clifford D. Taffet
Director of Rehabilitation
Dept. of Housing & Urban Devel.
802 Laura Street
Jacksonville, FL 32202
(904) 630-3400

Florida, Lee County
Mr. Dennis Simon
Community Development Director
P.O. Box 398
Fort Myers, FL 33902
(813) 335-2485

Florida, Palm Beach County
Ms. Cynthia Matthews
Housing Manager
Div. of Housing & Community Devel.
Palm Beach County
802 Evernia Street
West Palm Beach, FL 33401
(407) 641-3264

Florida, Pensacola
Mr. William D. Chiles
Housing Administrator
City of Pensacola
P.O. Box 12910
Pensacola, FL 32521
(904) 435-1665

Florida, Pompano Beach
Mr. James Hudson
Coordinator of Community Devel.
City of Pompano Beach Planning
Department
Community Development Division
Post Office Drawer 1300
Pompano Beach, FL 33061
(305) 786-4651

Forida, St. Petersburg
Ms. Sally Trocki
Supervisor, Property Rehab.
Urban Redevelopment Agency
P.O. Box 2842
St. Petersburg, FL 33731
(813) 893-7284

Florida, Tampa
Mr. Fernando Noriega
Redevelopment Div. Manager
1310 9th Avenue
Tampa, FL 33605
(813) 223-8146

Georgia, Atlanta
Ms. Muriel Mitchell
Bureau of Housing & Redevelopment
236 Forsythe Street, S.W.
Suite 300
Atlanta, GA 30303
(404) 330-6410

Georgia, Savannah
Mr. Don Phoenix
Housing Grants
P.O. Box 1027
Savannah, GA 31402
(912) 651-6520

Idaho, Boise
Mr. Tim Hogland
Director, Building Department
P.O. Box 500
Boise, ID 83701
(208) 384-4430

Illinois, Aurora
Mr. Bill Wiet, Director
Div. of Neighborhood Redevel.
44 East Downer Place
Aurora, IL 60507
(708) 844-3623

Illinois, Chicago
Ms. Juanita Parrott
Supervisor, Loan Processing
318 South Michigan Avenue
Chicago, IL 60604
(312) 922-7922, ext. 535

Illinois, Decatur
Ms. Rolanda Johnson
Renewal Coordinator
Dept. of Community Development
One Civic Center Plaza
Decatur, IL 62523
(217) 424-2778

Illinois, East St. Louis
Ms. Carlyn Brooks
Div. Admin. of Urban Conservation
301 East Broadway
East St. Louis, IL 62201
(618) 482-6645

Illinois, Harvey
Mr. Stephen Heath
Rehabilitation Specialist
Dep. of Building Planning
15320 Broadway Avenue
Harvey, IL 60426
(708) 339-4200, ext. 38

Illinois, Joliet
Mr. Robert Listner, Director
Neighborhood Services Div.
City Hall
150 West Jefferson Street
Joliet, IL 60431
(815) 740-2455

Illinois, Kankakee
Mr. Charles Betterton
Finance Specialist
Community Development Agency
385 Oak Street
Kankakee, IL 60901
(815) 933-0506

Illinois, Rock Island
Mr. Alan Carmen
Housing Coordinator
Community Planning & Economic
Development Department
1528 3rd Avenue
Rock Island, IL 61201
(309) 793-3350

Illinois, Rockford
Ms. Vicki Manson
Neighborhood Dev. Coordinator
Dept. of Community Development
City Hall
425 East State Street
Rockford, IL 61104
(815) 987-5690

Indiana, Gary
Mrs. Nancy Valentine
Chief Homestead Officer
Dept. of Housing Conservation
824 Broadway
Gary, IN 46402
(219) 883-3102

Indiana, Indianapolis
Ms. Julia Beverley, Assistant Manager
Housing Operations
Economic & Housing Development
Dept. of Metropolitan Development
148 East Market St., 6th Floor
Indianapolis, IN 46204
(317) 633-3480

Indiana, Lake County
Mr. Richard Hucker, Director
Community & Economic Devel. Dep.
2293 North Main Street
Crown Point, IN 46307
(219) 755-3231

Indiana, South Bend
Mr. Theodore Leverman
Assistant Director
Urban Homesteading
Bureau of Housing
521 North Eclipse Place
South Bend, IN 46628
(219) 284-9475

Indiana, Terre Haute
Mr. Mike Kass
Housing Administrator
Department of Redevelopment
301 City Hall
17 Harding Avenue
Terre Haute, IN 47807
(812) 232-0018

Iowa, Cherokee
Mr. Michael Farris
City of Davenport
City Hall
226 West Fourth Street
Davenport, IA 52801
(319) 326-7748

Iowa, Des Moines
Mr. Richard Wright
Armory Building
East 1st and Des Moines
Des Moines, IA 50307
(515) 283-4180

Iowa, Sioux City
Ms. Louie Anderson
Rehab. Loan Officer
Community Development Dept.
P.O. Box 447
Sioux City, IA 51102
(712) 279-6277

Kansas, Kansas City
Mr. Ed Smith
Community Development Director
701 North Seventh Street, Room 823
Kansas City, KS 66101
(913) 573-5100

Kansas, Topeka
Mr. Chris Imming
Dept. of Housing and Community
Development
820 South Quincy, Suite 501
Topeka, KS 66612
(913) 234-0072

Kentucky, Jefferson County
Mr. Fred McMahon
Homestead Coordinator
Urban Government Center
810 Barrett Avenue, Room 621
Lousiville, KY 40202
(502) 625-6550

Kentucky, Louisville
Ms. Marcia Miller
Urban Homesteading Coordinator
Department of Housing
745 West Main Street
Louisville, KY 40202
(502) 625-3034

Louisiana, New Orleans
Mr. Joel Rochan
Office of Housing & Community Dev.
2400 Canal Street
New Orleans, LA 70119
(504) 589-7208

Louisiana, Shreveport
Mr. David Lewis
Neighborhood Housing Services
3034 Lakeshore Drive
Shreveport, LA 71133-6889
(318) 631-0161

Maryland, Prince George's County
Ms. Edna Kryzaniak
Dept. of Housing & Community Dev.
Landover Mall East
Promenade One, Suite 300
2103 Brightseat Road
Landover, MD 20785
(301) 925-5570

Michigan, Flint
Mr. Ed Custer
Project Manager
Flint Neighborhood Improvement
1101 South Saginaw
Flint, MI 48502
(313) 766-7428

Michigan, Genesee County
Mr. Thomas Georgen
Principal Planner
County of Genesee
1101 Beach Street, Room 214
Flint, MI 48602-1470
(313) 257-3010

Michigan, Grand Rapids
Mr. Steve Smith
Rehabilitation Supervisor
Rehabilitation Department
345 State Street
Grand Rapids, MI 49503
(616) 456-3132

Michigan, Inkster
Mr. Clarence Oden, Deputy Director
Community Development Dept.
2121 Inkster Road
Inkster, MI 48141
(313) 563-9761

Michigan, Jackson
Mr. Duane Miller
Urban Homesteading Coordinator
City of Jackson
161 West Michigan Avenue
Jackson, MI 49201
(517) 788-4187

Michigan, Kalamazoo
Ms. Peggy Giem
Grants Program Specialist
Housing & Programs Division
241 West South Street
Kalamazoo, MI 49007-4796
(616) 385-8225

Michigan, Lansing
Ms. Sandra Hearns
Development Division
Dept. of Planning & Municipal
Development
City of Lansing
119 North Washington Square
Lansing, MI 48933
(517) 759-1535

Michigan, Saginaw
Ms. Rosetta Havrell
Urban Homesteading Coordinator
Dept. of Neighborhood Services
City of Saginaw
1315 South Washington Avenue
City Hall
Saginaw, MI 48601
(517) 776-1535

Minnesota, Anoka County
Ms. Jo Ann Wright
CDBG Coordinator
Anoka County
Anoka County Courthouse
325 East Main Street
Anoka, MN 55303
(612) 421-4760, ext. 1178
(Serves Anoka & Columbia Heights)

Minnesota, Dakota County
Mr. Mark Ulfers, Project Manager
Dakota County HRA
2496 - 145th Street West
Rosemont, MN 55068
(612) 423-4800
(Serves Farmington, Hastings,
Lakeville, Rosemount, and West St.
Paul)

Minnesota, Duluth
Ms. Pam Kramer
City of Duluth
407 City Hall
Duluth, MN 55802-1199
(218) 723-3357

Minnesota, Minneapolis
Ms. Linda Larsen, Manager
Single Family Development
Minneapolis Development Agency
331 2nd Avenue, South, Suite 900
Minneapolis, MN 55401
(612) 342-1332

Minnesota, Rochester
Mr. Randy Klement
Rehab. Coordinator
Housing & Redev. Authority
2122 Campus Drive, S.E.
Rochester, MN 55094
(507) 285-8224

Minnesota, St. Cloud
Ms. Connie Mangan
Community Devel. Coordinator
St. Cloud Housing & Redev.
Authority
619 Germain Mall, Suite 212
St. Cloud, MN 56301
(612) 252-0880

32

Minnesota, St. Paul
Mr. Warren Frost, Project Manager
Dept. of Planning & Economic Dev.
25 West Fourth Street
City Hall Annex, 12th Floor
St. Paul, MN 55102
(612) 228-3361

Missouri, Berkeley
Mr. Bill Luchini
Community Development Dir.
City of Berkeley
6140 North Kanley Road
Berkeley, MO 63134
(314) 524-3313, ext. 149

Missouri, Ferguson
Ms. Deane Wagner, Director
Community Development
City of Ferguson
110 Church Street
Ferguson, MO 63135
(314) 521-7721

Missouri, Jennings
Ms. Jan Winfield
Housing Coordinator
City of Jennings
2120 Hord Avenue
Jennings, MO 63136
(314) 388-1164

Missouri, Kansas City
Ms. Deborah Williams
Dept. of Housing & Community Dev.
City Hall, 14th Floor
414 East 12th Street
Kansas City, MO 64104
(816) 274-2201

Missouri, Pine Lawn
Ms. Doris Jackson, Administrator
City of Pine Lawn
6250 Steve Marre Street
Pine Lawn, MO 63121
(314) 261-5500

Montana, Billings
Mr. John Walsh
Block Grant Manager
Community Development Dept.
P.O. Box 1178
Billings, MT 59103
(406) 657-8286

Nebraska, Omaha
Mr. Mike Sakler
Planning Department
Omaha-Douglas Civic Center
1819 Farnam Street, Rm. 1111
Omaha, NE 68183
(402) 444-5170

New Jersey, Camden
Mr. Stanley Witkowski
Housing Coordinator
Division of Housing Services
City Hall, Room 222
6th and Market Street
Camden, NJ 08101
(609) 757-7283

New York, Niagra Falls
Mr. William K. Clark
Community Development Dir.
City of Niagara Falls
City Hall, 745 Main Street
Niagara Falls, NY 14302
(716) 286-4470

Ohio, Canton
Ms. Sheila Barrino
Staff Coordinator
Housing & Neighborhood Devel.
221 3rd, S.E.
Canton, OH 44702
(216) 489-3258

Ohio, Cincinatti
Mr. Mike Hunley, Program Director
Neighborhood Housing
415 Court Street
Cincinnati, OH 45203
(513) 352-3743

Ohio, Cleveland
Ms. Barbara Hayes
Urban Homesteading Coordinator,
Rehabilitation Division
Dept. of Community Development
Cleveland City Hall
601 Lakeside Avenue
Cleveland, OH 44114
(216) 664-4105

Ohio, Cuyahoga County
Ms. Mary Jo Rawlins
Assistant Manager, Rehab.
Cuyahoga County
112 Hamilton
Cleveland, OH 44114
(216) 443-7260

Ohio, Dayton
Mr. Robert Murray
Senior Housing Specialist
City-Wide Development Corp.
Miami Valley Tower
40 West Fourth Street, Suite 1400
Dayton, OH 45402
(513) 226-0457

Ohio, Lima
Mr. Richard S. Schroeder
Director of Planning
City of Lima
219 East Market Street
Lima, OH 45801
(419) 228-5462

Ohio, Montgomery County
Ms. Judith Damico, Director
Montgomery County Corp.
1700 Miami Valley Tower
40 West Fourth Street
Dayton, OH 45402
(513) 225-6328

Ohio, Springfield
Mr. John Platt
Rehabilitation Coordinator
Development Department
76 East High Street
Springfield, OH 45502
(513) 324-7662

Ohio, Toledo
Mr. Bill Sullivan
Acting Conservation Officer
Dept. of Community Development
1 Government Center, Suite 1800
Toledo, OH 43604
(419) 245-1400

Ohio, Warren
Mr. John Foley, Director
Community Development Dept.
418 South Main Avenue
Warren, OH 44481
(216) 841-2595

Ohio, Youngstown
Mr. Don Weekly, Housing Director
Community Development Agency
496 Glenwood Avenue
Youngstown, OH 44502
(216) 746-8416

Oklahoma, Enid
Ms. Jan Webber
City of Enid
P.O. Box 1768
Enid, OK 73702
(405) 234-0400

Oklahoma, Lawton
Mr. Frank Pondrom
Homesteading Coordinator
103 South 4th Street
Lawton, OK 73501
(405) 581-3340

34

Oklahoma, Oklahoma City
Mr. Al Behrens, Interim Director
Dept. of Housing & Community Svc.
609 West Sheridan
Oklahoma City, OK 73102
(405) 231-2514

Oklahoma, Shawnee
Mr. Al Nix, Program Manager
P.O. Box 1448
Shawnee, OK 74801
(405) 273-1938

Oklahoma, Tulsa
Ms. Bobbie Cunningham
Urban Homesteading Coordinator
Dept. of City Development
1436 North Cincinatti
Tulsa, OK 74106
(918) 596-7777

Oregon, Malheur County
Ms. Merlene Bourasa
Urban Homesteading Coordinator
Housing Authority of Malheur County
308 East 2nd Street
Nyssa, OR 97913
(503) 372-5658

Oregon, Portland
Ms. Jennifer Gardiner
Acting Program Coordinator
Portland Development Commission
1425 N.E. Irving, Suite 200
Portland, OR 97232
(503) 823-3400

Pennsylvania, Allegheny County
Mr. George Arendas
Manager, Housing Division
Dept. of Development
400 Fort Pitt Commons
445 Fort Pitt Boulevard
Pittsburgh, PA 15219
(215) 644-1025

Pennsylvania, Allentown
Mr. Raymond Polaski
Director, Bureau of Code
Enforcement & Rehab.
Public Safety Building
435 Hamilton Street, Room 20
Allentown, PA 18101
(215) 437-7695

Pennsylvania, Chester
Mr. Stephen A. Merriken
Chester Redevelopment Authority
401 Avenue of the States
P.O. Box 437
Chester, PA 19016
(215) 447-7881

Pennsylvania, Delaware County
Mr. Edward Coleman, Exec. Director
Community Action Agency of
Delaware County
Government Center
2nd & Orange Streets
Media, PA 19063
(215) 891-5101

Pennsylvania, McKeesport
Mr. Dennis Pittman
Community Development Director
201 Lysle Boulevard
McKeesport, PA 15132
(412) 675-5080

Pennsylvania, Philadelphia
Mr. Jeffrey Allegretti
Director, Urban Homesteading
Philadelphia Housing Devel. Corp.
1234 Market Street, Room 440
Philadelphia, PA 19107
(215) 448-3151

Puerto Rico, Bayamon
Mr. Eduardo Nevarez
Planning Office
Municipality of Bayamon
Box 1588
Bayamon, PR 00619
(809) 740-6170

Puerto Rico, Ceiba
Ms. Claribel Feliciano
Ceiba Housing and Economic
Development Corp.
Box 203
Ceiba, PR 00635
(809) 885-3020

South Carolina, Anderson
Mr. Jerry Knighton, Jr.
Director of Community Devel. Dept.
City of Columbia
P.O. Box 147
Columbia, SC 29217
(803) 733-8313

South Carolina, Greenville County
Mr. Troy Newman
Acquisition and Relocation Specialist
Greenville County Redevel. Authority
301 University Ridge, Suite 2500
Greenville, SC 29601
(803) 242-9801

Tennessee, Chattanooga
Mr. David Fromm
Chattanooga Neighborhood
Enterprises, Inc.
615 Lindsay Street
Chattanooga, TN 37402
(615) 265-4114

Tennessee, Shelby County
Ms. Tommie Cervetti
Mangager, Housing
Dept. of Neighborhoods
Housing & Economic Development
204 North 2nd Street-Basement
Memphis, TN 38105
(901) 576-3730

Texas, Fort Worth
Mr. Stephen Johnson
Homesteading Coordinator
Housing & Human Services Dept.
Fort Worth Housing Financial Corp.
1000 Throckmorton
Fort Worth, TX 76102
(817) 870-7377

Texas, Houston
Mr. Cele Quesada
Houston Housing Financial Corp.
P.O. Box 1562
Houston, TX 77251
(713) 247-1251

Texas, Lubbock
Ms. Sandy Ogletree
Community Development Admin.
P.O. Box 2000
Lubbock, TX 79457
(806) 762-6411, ext. 2290

Texas, San Antonio
Mr. Andrew Cameron
Community Development Office
P.O. Box 839966
San Antonio, TX 78283
(512) 299-8299

Utah, Salt Lake City
Mr. Ron Pohlman
SLC Redevelopment Agency
285 West North Temple, Suite 200
Salt Lake City, Utah 84103
(801) 328-3211

Utah, Salt Lake County
Mr. John Godfrey
Rehabilitation Director
Housing Authority of Salt Lake
County
1962 South 200 East Street
Salt Lake City, Utah 84115
(801) 487-0191

Washington, Richland
Mr. Vieno Lindstrom, Supervisor
City of Richland
P.O. Box 190
Richland, WA 99352
(509) 943-9161

Washington, Spokane
Ms. Linda Storms
Northwest Regional Foundation
E. 525 Mission
Spokane, WA 99202
(509) 483-4663

Washington, Yakima
Ms. Dixie Kracht
Housing Supervisor
CDBG Manager
112 South 8th Street
Yakima, WA 98901
(509) 575-6101

Wisconsin, Kenosha
Mr. Mitch Engen
Urban Homesteading Coordinator
Dept. of City Development
625 52nd Street
Kenosha, WI 53140
(414) 656-8055

Wisconsin, Milwaukee
Mr. John Worm, Homestead Manager
Dept. of City Development
809 North Broadway
Milwaukee, WI 53202
(414) 223-5607

Wisconsin, Racine
Mr. Thomas Wright
Dept. of City Development
City of Racine
730 Washington Avenue
Racine, WI 53403
(414) 636-9151

Local Contacts
State Programs

Georgia, State of
Mr. Tom Gladis
Georgia Residential Finance
Authority
60 Executive Parkway South, Suite 250
Atlanta, GA 30329
(404) 679-4840

Ohio, State of
Mr. Stanley Turner, Exec. Director
Spring, Inc.
Arcue Building, Suite 707
6 West High Street
Springfield, OH 45502
(513) 323-7997

Wyoming, State of
Mr. George Axlund
Executive Director
Wyoming Comm. Devel. Authority
123 South Durbin Street
Casper, WY 82602
(307) 265-0603
(Serves Casper and Glenrock)

7.0 THE DEPARTMENT OF HOUSING AND URBAN DEVELOPMENT (HUD)

The United States Congress has mandated the Department of Housing and Urban Development to create conditions for every family in the U.S. to have decent and affordable housing. Additionally, they require equal housing opportunity for all, with the desire to strengthen and enrich our country's communities.

Under Jack Kemp's leadership (he is currently the secretary for HUD), the following priorities have been set:

(1)   The expansion of homeownerhsip and affordable housing opportunities.

(2)   The creation of jobs and economic development through Enterprise Zones.

(3)   Empowering the poor through Resident Management programs and homesteading.

(4)   The enforcement of fair housing for all.

(5)   Assisting in making public housing drug free.

(6)   Assisting in turning the tide on the plight of the homeless in the U.S.

Through the Department of Housing and Urban Development, our government owns anywhere from 10,000 to 50,000 properties at any given time throughout the U.S. When these properties are repossessed, they are made available to the general public for sale. HUD homes usually sell below market value. An additional advantage of purchasing a HUD home is that the interest rates are favorable and the transfer fees and other closing costs are minimal.

Some houses listed for bid come in "as is" condition, which means there are no warranties on the property, and that it is not eligible for FHA financing. Like the Urban Homesteading houses, you are required to bring these homes up to code yourself.

Following is a brief overview of the HUD programs currently in effect. Many of these are discussed in greater detail in subsequent chapters.

7.1   Community Development Block Grants — (Entitlement)

Provides Federal aid to promote sound community development.

This program provides annual Community Development Block Grants (CDBG) on a formula basis to entitled communities to carry out a wide range of community development activities which are aimed at neighborhood revitalization, economic development, and improved community facilities and services.

All CDBG activities must benefit low and moderate income families, or aid the prevention or elimination of slums; or address other community development needs that present a serious and immediate threat to the health or welfare of the community. Some of the activities that can be carried out with community development funds include the purchase of real property; rehabilitation of residential and non-residential properties; provision of public facilities and improvements (such as water, sewer, streets and neighborhood centers); and assistance to profit-motivated business to help with economic development activities in a given community.

Not less than 60 percent of the funds must be used for activities which benefit low and moderate income persons.

Metropolitan cities and urban counties are entitled to receive annual grants. The amount of each entitlement grant is determined by statutory formula which uses several objective measures of community need, which include poverty, population, housing overcrowding, age of housing, and growth lag.

These grants are administered by the Assistant Secretary for Community Planning and Development, Department of Housing and Urban Development, Washington, D.C. 20410-7000. You can obtain additional information at your local HUD office or at a field office.

7.2 **Community Development Block Grants (Non-entitlement) For States And Small Cities.**

This program provides grants to carry out a wide range of community development activities directed toward neighborhood revitalization, economic development, and improved community facilities and services. Applicants are required to give maximum priority to activities which will aid in the prevention or elimination of slums. As with the previously mentioned grants, no less than 60% of the funds must be used for activities which benefit low and moderate income families.

Under the 1981 amendments to the Community Development Block Grant legislation, each state has the option to administer the block grant funds provided for its non-entitlement areas.

If this option is exercised, the block grant funds are provided to the states which distribute them as grants to the eligible units of general local government. The states' objectives and methods of distributing the funds are determined by working with citizens in the community who will be affected, and local elected officials. Each state must report annually on how the funds were used.

All fifty states and Puerto Rico are eligible to apply to distribute funds to non-entitlement units of government, usually under 50,000 in population, that are not metropolitan cities or part of an urban county.

The Assistant Secretary for Community Planning and Development, Department of Housing and Urban Development, Washington D.C., 20410-7000 handles these grants. If you want information, you can contact your local officials or a HUD field office.

7.3 **Community Development Block Grants (Section 108 Loan Guarantee)**

Section 108 is the loan guarantee provision of the Community Development Block Grant (CDBG) program. It provides communities with front-end financing for large-scale community and economic development projects that cannot be financed from annual grants.

Eligible activities are:

(a)   acquisition of real property;
(b)   rehabilitation of publicly owned real property;
(c)   housing rehabilitation;
(d)   economic development activities eligible under the CDBG program; and
(e)   related relocation, clearance, and site improvements.

The CDBG rules and requirements apply for the purposes of determining eligibility. As with the CDBG program, all projects and activities must either principally benefit low and moderate income persons, aid in the elimination of slums, or meet other community development needs having a particular urgency.

Loan guarantees under Section 108 are subject to a statutory maximum equal to three times the applicant's annual entitlement amount.

The principal security for the loan guarantee is a pledge by the applicant of its current and future CDBG funds. HUD may also require additional security to be furnished if it is deemed necessary.

Metropolitan cities and urban counties that receive entitlement grants are eligible for Section 108. Once again, the administering office is the same as for the block grants, and you can get that information from HUD Headquarters and field offices.

7.4   **Rental Rehabilitation**

Rental rehabilitation provides grants to cities and states encourage rental housing rehabilitation, and rental subsidies to help lower income tenants remain in the building or relocate to other suitable housing. This program is designed to minimize displacement and attract private financing for rehabilitation.

These grants are awarded on a formula basis to communities of 50,000 or greater population, urban counties, and state, as well as with additional housing vouchers the local Public Housing Authority.

Rental Rehab funds (generally not more than an average of $5,000 to $8,500 per unit) may be used for up to one-half the total, eligible, rehabilitation costs of the project. An average minimum rehabilitation of $600 per unit is required to assure that a certain level of rehabilitation is necessary before public subsidies are provided.

Eligible rehabilitation activities are limited by the Act to those necessary to correct substandard conditions, make essential improvements, and repair major systems in danger of failure. Energy-related repairs considered necessary by the grantee, as well as those repairs necessary to make rental units accessible to the handicapped are also eligible.

After rehab, 70 to 100 percent of the units in a local program must be occupied by low-income families. In addition, an equitable share of grant funds must be used to aid large families. Rents after rehabilitation must be at market rates and not limited by rent controls.

Grants may be used only in neighborhoods where the median income does not exceed 80 percent of the area median, and where rents are not likely to increase more rapidly than the market area.

HUD will award funds based on a formula which considers three specific factors:

(1)   Rental units where the income of rental households is at or below the poverty level.

(2)   Rental units built before 1940, where the income of the household is at or below the poverty level; and

(3)   Rental units with at least one of four housing problems — overcrowding, high rent costs, incomplete kitchen facilities, or incomplete plumbing. This factor is weighted double in the formula.

If a state does not elect to administer its share of Rental Rehab funds, HUD will award funds to eligible grantees through a competitive program. The same contacts and addresses apply for this program as with the block grants.

7.5   One-to-four Family Home Mortgage Insurance (Section 203)

This program provides federal mortgage insurance to finance homeownership and the construction and financing of housing.

By insuring commercial lenders against loss, HUD encourages them to invest capital in the home mortgage market. HUD insures loans made by private financial institutions for up to 97% of the property value and for terms of up to 30 years. The loan may finance homes in both urban and rural areas (except for farm houses). Less rigid construction standards are permitted in rural areas.

HUD/FHA insured homeowners threatened with foreclosure due to circumstances beyond their control, such as job loss, death, or illness in the family, may apply for assignment of the mortgage to HUD which, if it accepts assignment, takes over the mortgage and adjusts the mortgage payments for a period of time until the homeowners can resume their financial responsibilities.

Any person able to meet the cash investment, the mortgage payments and the credit requirements is eligible.

This program is administered by the Assistant Secretary for Housing Federal Housing Commissioner, Department of Housing and Urban Development, Washington, D.C. 20410-8000. You can obtain additional information from a HUD Field Office.

7.6   Homeownership Assistance for Low and Moderate Income Families (Section 221(d)(2))

This program is designed to provide mortgage insurance to increase homeownership opportunities for low and moderate income families, especially those displaced by urban renewal.

HUD insures lenders against loss on mortgage loans to finance the purchase, construction, or rehabilitation of low-cost, one-to-four family housing. Maximum insurable loans for an owner-occupant are $31,000 for a single-family home (up tp $36,000 in high-cost areas). For a larger family (five or more persons), the limits are $36,000 or up to $42,000 in high-cost areas. Higher mortgage limits apply to two-to-four family housing.

Anyone is eligible to apply, but special consideration is given to displaced households.

If you are interested in further information, the same address applies for this program as in Section 203.

7.7 Housing In Declining Neighborhoods (Section 223(e))

This program is designed to provide mortgage insurance to purchase or rehabilitate housing in older, declining urban areas.

To handle the need for adequate housing for low and moderate income families, HUD insures lenders against loss on mortgage loans to finance the purchase, rehabilitation, or construction of housing in older, declining, but still viable urban areas where conditions are such that normal requirements for mortgage insurance cannot be met. The property must be in a reasonably viable neighborhood and an acceptable risk under the mortgage insurance rules. The terms of the loans are according to the HUD/FHA program under which the mortgage is insured. HUD determines if a project should be insured under Section 223(e) and become an obligation of Special Risk Insurance Fund. This is not a separate program; it supplements other HUD mortgage insurance because your property is located in an older, declining urban area.

The same addresses apply as previously mentioned for Section 203 and 221(d).

7.8 Special Credit Risks (Section 237)

This program provides mortgage insurance and homeownership counseling for low and moderate income families with a credit history that does not qualify them for insurance under normal underwriting standards.

HUD insures lenders against loss on home mortgage loans to low and moderate income families that are marginal credit risks. HUD is also authorized to provide budget, debt-management, and related counseling services to these families when needed. These services are performed by local HUD-approved organizations. Applicants may seek credit assistance under most FHA home mortgage insurance programs. Insured mortgage limit is $18,000 ($21,000 in high-cost areas).

Low and moderate income households with credit records indicating ability to manage their financial and other affairs successfully if given budget, debt-management, and related counseling are eligible.

You can check with your local HUD Field Office for further information on this program.

7.9   Condominium Housing (Section 234)

This program provides federal mortgage insurance to finance the construction or rehabilitation or multi-family housing by sponsors who intend to sell individual units and to finance acquisition costs of individual units in proposed or existing condominiums.

HUD insures mortgages made by private lending institutions for the purchase of individual family units in multi-family housing projects. Sponsors may also obtain FHA-insured mortgages to finance the construction or rehabilitation of housing projects which they intend to sell as individual condominium units. A project must contain at least four dwelling units; they may be a detached, semi-detached, row, walk-up, or elevator structure.

A condominium is defined as joint ownership of common areas and facilities by the separate owners of single dwelling units in the project.

Any qualified profit-motivated or nonprofit sponsor may apply for a blanket mortgage covering the project after conferring with his/her local HUD-FHA Field Office; any creditworthy person may apply for a mortgage on individual units in a project.

7.10   Manufactured Homes (Title 1)

HUD insures loans to finance the purchase of manufactured homes and/or lots. The loans are made by private lending institutions. The maximum loan amount is $40,500 for a manufactured home, $54,000 for a manufactured home plus a suitably developed lot, and $12,500 for a developed lot. The maximum limits for combination home-and-lot loans may be increased up to 50 percent in designated high-cost areas. The maximum loan term varies from 15 to 25 years, depending upon the type of loan.

Any person able to make the cash investment and the mortgage payments is eligible.

You can talk to your Regional HUD office for further details.

7.11   Manufactured Home Parks (Section 207)

HUD insures mortgages made by private lending institutions to help finance construction or rehabilitation of manufactured home parks consisting of five or more spaces. Mortgages are limited to $9,000 per individual manufactured home space within each park. In high-cost areas, this maximum may be increased to $15,750 per space. The park must be located in an area approved by HUD in which market conditions show a need for such housing.

Investors, builders, developers, cooperatives, and others meeting HUD requirements are eligible to apply to an FHA-approved lending institution after conferring with the local HUD office.

7.12   Existing Multi-family Rental Housing (Section 223(f))

HUD insures mortgages to purchase or refinance existing multi-family projects originally financed with or without Federal mortgage insurance. HUD may insure mortgages on existing multi-family projects under this program that do not require substantial rehabilitation. The project must contain at least five units and must be at least three years old.

Investors, builders, developers, and others who meet HUD requirements are eligible.

Additional information can be obtained by contacting your HUD field office.

7.13   Multi-family Rental Housing for Moderate-income Families (Section 221(d) (3) and (4))

HUD insures mortgages made by private lending institutions to help finance construction or substantial rehabilitation of MULTI-FAMILY (five or more units) rental or cooperative housing for moderate-income or displaced families. Projects in both cases may consist of detached, semi-detached, row, walk-up, or elevator structures.

Currently, the principal difference between the programs is that HUD may insure up to 100% of total project cost under Section 221(d)(3) for nonprofit and cooperative mortgagors, but only up to 90% under Section 221(d)(4), regardless of the type of mortgagor.

These mortgages may be obtained by public agencies; nonprofit, limited-dividend, or cooperative organizations; private builders; or investors who sell completed projects to such organizations. Section 221(d)(4) mortgages may be obtained by profit-motivated sponsors. Tenant occupancy is not restricted by income limits.

Your nearest HUD Field Office will have additional information for you.

7.14   Assistance to Nonprofit Sponsors of Low and Moderate Income Housing (Section 106)

This program provides technical assistance and loans to sponsors of certain HUD-assisted housing.

It is provided to stimulate the production of housing for low and moderate income families.

HUD also makes interest-free "seed money" loans to nonprofit sponsors or public housing agencies to cover 80% of the preliminary development costs. Current HUD regulations limit these loans to nonprofit sponsors of Section 202 housing for the elderly or handicapped. Loans may be used to meet typical project development costs, such as surveys and market analysis, site engineering, architectural fees, site option expenses, legal fees, consultant fees, and organization expenses.

Nonprofit sponsors eligible under HUD regulations to participate in the Section 202 program are eligible for this program. You can obtain additional information from you nearest HUD Field Office.

7.15   Rent Supplements

This program provides federal payment to reduce rents for certain disadvantaged low-income persons.

HUD may pay rent supplements on behalf of eligible tenants to certain private owners of multi-family housing insured by the FHA. The payment makes up the difference between 30% of the tenant's adjusted income and the fair market rent determined by HUD. The subsidy may not exceed 70% of the HUD-approved rent for the specific unit. HUD may pay the supplements for a maximum term of 40 years.

To find out about eligibility, and for additional information contact your nearest HUD Field Office.

7.16   Lower-income Rental Assistance (Section 8)

This program assists low and very low income families in obtaining decent, safe, and sanitary housing in private accommodations.

HUD makes up the difference between what a low and very low income household can afford and the approved rent for an adequate housing unit. Eligible tenants must pay the highest of either 30% of adjusted income, 10% of gross income, or the portion of welfare assistance designated to meet housing costs. Housing subsidized in this way by HUD must meet certain standards of safety and sanitation, and rents for these units generally cannot exceed the fair market rents for these units as determined by HUD. This rental assistance may be used in existing housing, in new construction, and in moderately or substantially rehabilitated units.

Project sponsors may be private owners, profit-motivated and nonprofit or cooperative organizations, public housing agencies, and state housing finance agencies. Very low income families whose incomes do not exceed 50% of the median income for the area are eligible to occupy the assisted units. A limited number of available units may be rented to lower-income families whose incomes are between 50% and 80% of median.

Your nearest HUD Field Office can supply you with additional information.

7.17   Direct Loans for Housing for the Elderly or Handicapped (Section 202)

This program provides long-term direct loans to eligible, private nonprofit sponsors to finance rental or cooperative housing facilities for occupancy by elderly or handicapped persons. The interest rate is determined annually. Section 9 funds are made available for 100% of the Section 202 units for the elderly. Beginning in Fiscal Year 1989, rental assistance was provided for 100% of the units for handicapped people.

Private, nonprofit sponsors may qualify for loans. Households of one or more persons, the head of which is at least 62 years old, or is qualified as nonelderly handicapped between the ages of 18 and 62, are eligible to live in the structures.

Once again, you need to contact your nearest HUD Field Office to find out about programs in your area.

7.18   Property Improvement Loan Insurance (Title 1)

HUD insures loans to finance improvements, alterations, and repairs of private homes, apartment buildings, and non-residential structures. Also, loans may finance new construction of nonresidential buildings. Loans on single family homes and nonresidential structures may be for up to $17,500 and may extend to 15 years. Lenders process these loans. Loans for more than $2,500 require a mortgage or deed of trust on the improved property.

Eligibility is determined by the lender.

Contact your nearest HUD Regional Office for more information.

7.19 Graduated Payment Mortgages (Section 245)

Under this program, HUD insures mortgages to finance early homeownership for households that expect their incomes to rise substantially. The "graduated payment" mortgages allow homeowners to make smaller monthly payments initially and to increase the size of their payment gradually over time.

Five different plans are available, varying in length and rate of increase. Larger than usual down payments are required to prevent the total amount of the loan from exceeding the statutory loan-to-value ratios. In other words, the graduated payment mortgage is subject to the rules governing ordinary HUD-insured home loans.

All FHA approved lenders may make graduated payment mortgages; creditworthy applicants with reasonable expectations of increasing their income may qualify for these loans.

Your nearest HUD Field Office can provide you with additional information.

7.20 Adjustable Rate Mortgages (ARMS)

Under this HUD-insured mortgage, the interest rate and monthly payment may change during the life of the loan. The initial interest rate, discount points, and the margin are negotiable between the buyer and lender.

The one-year *Treasury Constant Maturities Index* is used for determining the interest rate changes. One percentage point is the maximum amount the interest rate may increase or decrease in any one year. Over the life of the loan, the maximum interest rate change is five percentage points from the initial rate of the mortgage.

Lenders are required to disclose to the borrower the nature of the ARM loan at the time of loan application. In addition, borrowers must be informed at least 30 days in advance of ANY adjustment to the monthly payment.

All FHA-approved lenders may make adjustable rate mortgages; creditworthy applicants who will be owner-occupants may qualify for these loans.

You can obtain additional information on this ARMS program by contacting your nearest HUD Field Office.

7.21 Joint Venture for Affordable Housing (JVAH)

The goal of the JVAH is affordable homeownerhsip and rentals for zero-income through middle-income Americans. By involving builders, developers, local governments, and others connected with the housing industry who are concerned with housing affordability, the JVAH creates affordable housing opportunities through regulatory reform, elimination of red tape, and the use of innovative construction and land planning techniques. It focuses on controllable factors contributing to housing costs, including deregulation and building code modification; enlists community organizations to work for housing affordability, helping them to launch their own affordable housing campaigns; and functions as a clearing house for resource materials and ideas.

Anyone (especially first-time homebuyers) able to meet the cash investment, the mortgage payments, and credit underwriting requirements is eligible for this program.

For further information you should contact:
Assistant Secretary for Housing-Federal Housing Commissioner
Department of Housing and Urban Development
Washington, D.C. 20410-8000

7.22 Counseling for Homebuyers, Homeowners and Tenants

The Department is authorized to counsel homebuyers, homeowners, and tenants under HUD programs. Services are provided by HUD-approved counseling agencies at no cost to individuals and families under HUD programs. HUD approves agencies and private and public organizations with competence, knowledge, and experience in housing counseling and Departmental programs. Housing counseling grants, when available, are awarded to HUD-approved counseling agencies, on a competitive basis, to reimburse them partially for costs.

Counseling consists of advising and assisting with budgeting, money management, and buying and maintaining a home. It includes referrals for financial assistance, food, medical care, family guidance, job training, and placement. Counseling services help homeowners and tenants to improve their housing conditions and meet their responsibilities.

Homebuyers, homeowners, and tenants under HUD programs are eligible for counseling; private and public nonprofit agencies may apply for HUD approval to provide housing counseling services.

Your nearest HUD Field Office can provide you with more information on this VERY worthwhile program! There are approximately 500 HUD-approved housing counseling agencies throughout the U.S.

These are just some of the many, many programs currently active through the U.S. Department of Housing and Urban Development. If you are contemplating the purchase of a home, you will definitely want to contact your nearest HUD office to gather information that applies to your situation. The following map and listings of Field Offices should give you a head start!

52

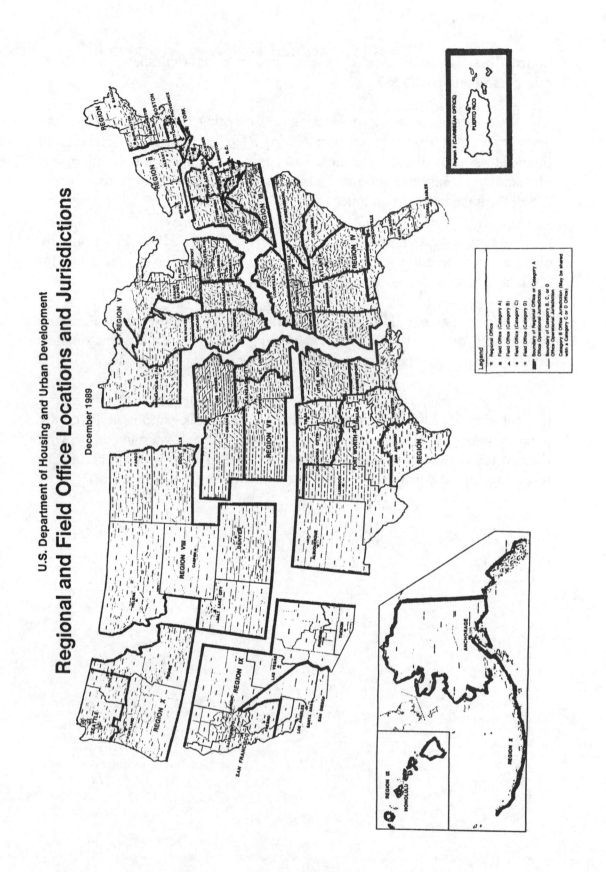

U.S. Department of Housing and Urban Development

Regional and Field Office Locations and Jurisdictions

December 1989

Field Office Addresses and Telephone Numbers

Region I (Boston)

Boston Regional Office
Room 375
Thomas P. O'Neill, Jr.
Federal Bldg.
10 Causeway Street
Boston, MA 02222-1092
Commerical No. (617) 565-5256

FIELD OFFICES

Bangor Office
First Floor
Casco Northern Bank Building
23 Main Street
Bangor, ME 04401-4318
Commerical No. (207) 945-0467

Burlington Office
Room B-31
Federal Building
11 Elmwood Ave.
P.O. Box 879
Burlington, VT 05402-0879
Commercial No. (802) 951-6290

Hartford Office
First Floor
330 Main Street
Hartford, Connecticut 06106-1860
Commercial No. (203) 240-4523

Manchester Office
Norris Cotton Federal Building
275 Chestnut Street
Manchester, NH 03101-2487
Commercial No. (603) 666-7681

Providence Office
330 John O. Pastore Federal
Building & and U.S. Post Office
Kennedy Plaza
Providence, RI 02903-1785
Commercial No. (401) 528-5351

Region II (New York)

New York Regional Office
26 Federal Plaza
New York, NY 10278-0068

Commercial No. (212) 264-6500

FIELD OFFICES

Albany Office
Leo W. O'Brien Federal Building
North Pearl Street & Clinton Ave.
Albany, NY 12207-2395
Commercial No. (518) 472-3567

Buffalo Office
Fifth Floor
Lafayette Court
465 Main Street
Buffalo, NY 14203-1780
Commercial No. (716) 846-5755

Camden Office
The Parkade Building
519 Federal Street
Camden, NJ 08103-9998
Commercial No. (609) 757-5081

Caribbean Office
New San Juan Office Building
159 Carlos Chardon Avenue
San Juan, PR 00918-1804
Commercial No. (809) 766-6121

Newark Office
Military Park Building
60 Park Place
Newark, NJ 07102-5504
Commercial No. (201) 877-1662

Region III (Philadelphia)

Philadelphia Regional Office
Liberty Square Building
105 South Seventh Street
Philadelphia, PA 19106-3392
Commercial No. (215) 597-2560

FIELD OFFICES

Baltimore Office
Third Floor
The Equitable Building
10 North Calvert Street
Baltimore, MD 21202-1865
Commercial No. (301) 962-2520

Charleston Office
Suite 708
405 Capitol Street
Charleston, WV 25301-1795
Commercial No. (304) 347-7000

Pittsburgh Office
412 Old Post Office Courthouse
7th Avenue and Grant Street
Pittsburgh, PA 15219-1906
Commercial No. (412) 644-6428

Richmond Office
First Floor
The Federal Building
400 North 8th Street
P.O. Box 10170
Richmond, VA 23240-0170
Commercial No. (804) 771-2721

Washington, D.C. Office
Room 3158
451 Seventh Street, SW
Washington, D.C. 20410-5500
Commercial No. (202) 708-1422

Wilmington Office
Room 1304
J. Caleb Boggs Federal Building
844 King Street
Wilmington, DE 19801-3519
Commercial No. (302) 573-6300

Region IV (Atlanta)

Atlanta Regional Office
Richard B. Russell Federal
Building
75 Spring Street, SW
Atlanta, GA 30303-3388
Commercial No. (404) 331-5136

FIELD OFFICES

Birmingham Office
Suite 300
Beacon Ridge Tower
600 Beacon Parkway, West
Birmingham, Al 35209-3144
Commercial No. (205) 290-7617

Columbia Office
Strom Thurmond Federal Building
1835-45 Assembly Street
Columbia, SC 29201-2480
Commercial No. (803) 765-5592

Coral Gables Office
Gables 1 Tower
1320 South Dixie Highway
Coral Gables, FL 33146-2911
Commercial No. (305) 662-4500

Greensboro Office
415 North Edgeworth Street
Greensboro, NC 27401-2107
Commercial No. (919) 333-5363

Jackson Office
Suite 910
Doctor A.H. McCoy Federal Bldg.
100 West Capitol Street
Jackson, MS 39269-1096
Commercial No. (601) 965-4752

Jacksonville Office
325 West Adams Street
Jacksonville, FL 32202-4303
Commercial No. (904) 791-2626

Knoxville Office
Third Floor
John J. Duncan Federal Building
710 Locust Street
Knoxville, TN 37902-2526
Commercial No. (615) 549-9384

Louisville Office
601 West Broadway
P.O. Box 1044
Lousiville, KY 40201-1044
Commercial No. (502) 582-5251

Memphis Office
Suite 1200
One Memphis Place
200 Jefferson Avenue
Memphis, TN 38103-2335
Commercial No. (901)-544-3367

Nashville Office
Suite 200
251 Cumberland Bend Drive
Nashville, TN 37228-1803
Commercial No. (615) 736-5233

Orlando Office
Suite 270
Langley Building
3751 Maguire Boulevard
Orlando, FL 32803-3032
Commercial No. (407) 648-6441

Tampa Office
Room 527
700 Twiggs Street
P.O. Box 172910
Tampa, FL 33672-2910
Commercial No. (813) 228-2501

Region V (Chicago)

Chicago Regional Office
626 West Jackson Boulevard
Chicago, IL 60606-5601
Commercial No. (312) 353-5680
and
547 West Jackson Boulevard
Chicago, IL 60606-5760
Commercial No. (312) 353-6236

FIELD OFFICES

Cincinatti Office
Room 9002
Federal Office Building
550 Main Street
Cincinnati, OH 45202-3253
Commercial No. (513) 684-2884

Cleveland Office
Room 420
One Playhouse Square
1375 Euclid Avenue
Cleveland, OH 44114-1670
Commercial No. (216) 522-4058

Columbus Office
200 North High Street
Columbus, OH 43215-2499
Commercial No. (614) 469-5737

Detroit Office
Patrick V. McNamara Fed. Bldg.
477 Michigan Avenue
Detroit, MI 48226-2592
Commercial No. (313) 226-6280

Flint Office
Room 200
Ameritech Building-Local
352 South Saginaw Street
Flint, MI 48502-1953
Commercial No. (313) 766-5109

Grand Rapids Office
2922 Fuller Avenue, NE
Grand Rapids, MI 49505-3409
Commercial No. (616) 456-2100

Indianapolis Office
151 North Delaware Street
Indianapolis, IN 46204-2526
Commercial No. (317) 226-6303

Milwaukee Office
Suite 1380
Henry S. Reuss Federal Plaza
310 West Wisconsin Avenue
Milwaukee, WI 53203-2289
Commercial No. (414) 297-3214

Minneapolis-St. Paul Office
220 Second Street, South
Minneapolis, MN 55401-2195
Commercial No. (612) 370-3000

Springfield Office
Suite 672
Lincoln Tower Plaza
524 South 2nd Street
Springfield, IL 62701-1774
Commercial No. (217) 492-4085

Region VI (Fort Worth)

Fort Worth Regional Office
1600 Throckmorton
Post Office Box 2905
Fort Worth, TX 76113-2905
Commercial No. (817) 885-5401

FIELD OFFICES

Albuquerque Office
625 Truman Street, NE
Albuquerque, NM 87110-6443
Commercial No. (505) 262-6463

Dallas Office
Room 860
525 Griffin Street
Dallas, TX 75202-5007
Commercial No. (214) 767-8359

Houston Office
Suite 200
Norfolk Tower
2211 Norfolk
Houston, TX 77098-4096
Commercial No. (713) 653-3274

Little Rock Office
Suite 200
Lafayette Building
523 Louisiana Street
Little Rock, AR 72201-3707
Commercial No. (501) 324-6296

Lubbock Office
Federal Office Building
1205 Texas Avenue
Lubbock, TX 79401-4093
Commercial No. (806) 743-7265

New Orleans Office
Fisk Federal Building
1661 Canal Street
New Orleans, LA 70112-2887
Commercial No. (504) 589-7200

Oklahoma City Office
Murrah Federal Building
200 N.W. Fifth Street
Oklahoma City, OK 73102-3202
Commercial No. (405) 231-4181

San Antonio Office
Washington Square
800 Dolorosa
San Antonio, TX 78207-4563
Commercial No. (512) 229-6800

Shreveport Office
New Federal Building
500 Fannin Street
Shreveport, LA 71101-3077
Commercial No. (318) 226-5385

Tulsa Office
Suite 110
Boston Place
1516 South Boston Street
Tulsa OK 74119-4032
Commercial No. (918) 744-1000

Region VII (Kansas City)

Kansas City Regional Office
Professional Building
1103 Grand Avenue
Kansas City, MO 64106-2496
Commercial No. (913) 236-2100

FIELD OFFICES

Des Moines Office
Room 239
Federal Building
210 Walnut Street
Des Moines, IA 50309-2155
Commercial No. (515) 284-4512

Omaha Office
Braiker/Brandeis Building
210 South 16th Street
Omaha, NE 68102-1622
Commercial No. (402) 221-3703

St. Louis Office
210 North Tucker Boulevard
St. Louis, MO 63101-1997
Commercial No. (314) 539-6583

Topeka Office
Room 256
Frank Carlson Federal Building
444 S.E. Quincy
Topeka, KS 66683-0001
Commercial No. (913) 295-2652

Region VIII (Denver)

Denver Regional Office
Executive Tower Building
1405 Curtis Street
Denver, CO 80202-2349
Commercial No. (303) 844-4513

FIELD OFFICES

Casper Office
4225 Federal Office Building
100 East B Street
P.O. Box 580
Casper, WY 82602-1918
Commercial No. (307) 261-5252

Fargo Office
Federal Building
653 2nd Avenue North
P.O. Box 2483
Fargo, ND 58108-2483
Commercial No. (701) 239-5136

Helena Office
Room 340
Federal Office Bldg, Drawer 10095
301 South Park
Helena, MT 59626-0095
Commercial No. (406) 449-5205

Salt Lake City Office
Suite 220
324 South State Street
Salt Lake City, UT 84111-2321
Commercial No. (801) 524-5379

57

Sioux Falls Office
Suite 116
"300" Building
300 North Dakota Avenue
Sioux Falls, SD 57102-0311
Commercial No. (605) 330-4223

Region IX (San Francisco)

San Francisco Regional Office
Phillip Burton Federal Building
and U.S. Courthouse
450 Golden Gate Avenue
P.O. Box 36003
San Francisco, CA 94102-3448
Commercial No. (415) 556-4752

Indian Programs Office, Region IX
Suite 400
1 North First Street
Phoenix, AZ 85004-2360
Commercial No. (602) 379-4156

FIELD OFFICES

Fresno Office
Suite 138
1630 E. Shaw Avenue
Fresno, CA 93710-8193
Commercial No. (209) 487-5033

Honolulu Office
Prince Jonah Federal Building
300 Ala Moana Boulevard
P.O. Box 50007
Honolulu, HI 96850-4991
Commercial No. (808) 541-1323

Las Vegas Office
Suite 205
1500 E. Tropicana Avenue
Las Vegas, NV 89119-6516
Commercial No. (702) 388-6500

Los Angeles Office
1615 W. Olympic Boulevard
Los Angeles, CA 90015-3801
Commerical No. (213) 251-7122

Phoenix Office
Third Floor
1 North First Street
P.O. Box 13468
Phoenix, AZ 85002-3468
Commercial No. (602) 261-4434

Reno Office
1050 Bible Way
P.O. Box 4700
Reno, NV 89505-4700
Commercial No. (702) 784-5356

Sacramento Office
Suite 200
777 12th Street
Sacramento, CA 95809-1997
Commercial No. (916) 551-1351

San Diego Office
Room 5-S-3
Federal Office Building
880 Front Street
San Diego, CA 92188-0100
Commercial No. (619) 557-5310

Santa Ana Office
Box 12850
34 Civic Center Plaza
Santa Ana, CA 92712-2850
Commercial No. (714) 836-2451

Tucson Office
Suite 410
100 North Stone Avenue
Tucson, AZ 85701-1467
Commercial No. (602) 670-6237

Region X (Seattle)

Seattle Regional Office
Arcade Plaza Building
1321 Second Avenue
Seattle, WA 98101-2054
Commercial No. (206) 442-5414

FIELD OFFICES

Anchorage Office
Federal Building, U.S. Courthouse
222 West 8th Avenue, #64
Anchorage, AK 99513-7537
Commercial No. (907) 271-4170

Boise Office
Federal Building, U.S. Courthouse
550 West Fort Street
P.O. Box 042
Boise, ID 83724-0420
Commercial No. (208) 334-1990

Portland Office
520 Southwest Sixth Avenue
Portland, OR 97204-1596
Commercial No. (503) 326-3498

Spokane Office
Eighth Floor East
Farm Credit Bank Building
West 601 First Avenue
Spokane, WA 99204-0317
Commercial No. (509) 353-2510

8.0 YOUR GUIDE TO SINGLE FAMILY HOME MORTAGE INSURANCE

FHA, which is a part of HUD, administers various single family *mortgage insurance programs*. These programs operate through FHA approved lending institutions which submit applications to have the property appraised and have the buyer's credit approved. These lenders fund the mortgage loans which the Department insures. *HUD does not make direct loans to help people buy houses.*

The single family coinsurance program (244) about which many people inquire, is a lender program that provides the lender with only 90% insurance against potential loss on the mortgage. This is a program designed to allow lenders to process applications more rapidly.

8.1 FHA Home Mortgage Insurance

There are not many people who are able to pay cash for their homes. Assisting in the financing of home purchases on a sound basis is one of the primary purposes of FHA.

Under the FHA system, a homebuyer makes a small downpayment and obtains a mortage for the balance of the purchase price. The mortgage loan is made by a bank, savings and loan association, mortgage company, insurance company, or other FHA approved lender, and is insured by the U.S. Department of Housing and Urban Development (HUD/FHA).

FHA mortgages are *not* government loans. HUD does not lend money or build homes. HUD mortgage insurance protects the lender against loss on the mortgage. The lender can therefore offer more liberal mortgage terms than the homebuyer might otherwise be able to obtain, and many families that could not otherwise afford to do so can purchase a home.

The steps involved in obtaining such a loan are: (1) find a house that you are interested in buying, (2) call various lenders, such as mortgage companies, savings and loans, banks, etc., which you find listed under "Mortgages" in the Yellow Pages, (3) when you have fund the lender offering the best terms for you (the lowest interest rate and discount points), arrange a meeting with a loan officer to fill out the application forms. You will work directly with the lender; the lender will take care of getting HUD's approval. (see page 200 for samples of various HUD loan forms).

Mortgages insured by HUD can be used to pay for building, buying, or improving homes and for refinancing existing indebtedness.

Any individual who has a satisfactory credit record, the cash needed at closing, and enough steady income to make the monthly mortgage payments without difficulty can be approved.

HUD sets no upper age limit for the borrower, nor does it say the borrower must have a certain income to buy a home at a certain price. Income is considered along with other factors that help HUD judge whether or not the borrower will be able to repay the mortgage. HUD's analysis of income is applied equally to all applicants and co-applicants regardless of race, creed, religion, sex or marital status.

When applying for the loan, you will go to a lender that HUD has approved to make insured mortgage loans. Names of HUD-approved lenders are generally listed in the Yellow Pages under "Mortgages".

If the lender is willing to make the loan, it provides the proper forms and helps you complete them. At the application interview, you will have to provide the lender with your most recent bank statement and pay stub, and allow the lender to copy a picture identification and proof of your social security number. You will be asked to pay an appraisal fee and a fee for a credit report.

There are two separate methods of processing FHA insured single family loans. The fastest method is called Direct Endorsement processing. Under this method, Direct Endorsement lenders are authorized by HUD to issue loan commitments without prior submission of paperwork to HUD.

The second method of processing is called HUD processing and requires the lender to submit paperwork to HUD prior to approval of the property and, in a separate step, prior to approval of the borrower. With this method, HUD makes the decision to approve the loan for insurance and issues the loan commitments.

The lender then arranges with the borrower to close the loan. The borrower deals directly with the lender. The *lender* handles the transaction with HUD.

8.2   Shopping for A Loan

The cost of borrowing money can vary *significantly* from one lender to another. You will be wise to comparison shop for your home loan. The most critical things to consider when comparing home loans are the INTEREST RATE, THE NUMBER OF POINTS, THE TERM, CLOSING COSTS, AND IF THE LENDER IS WILLING TO LOCK IN THE RATE.

HUD does not establish the interest rate or set either a maximum or minimum on the interest rate or on discount points that may be paid by the borrower. This means that a borrower can pay whatever interest rate and discount points, as well as any commitment fee, that the borrower and lender agree upon. The seller can pay the discount points, or a portion of them, if the buyer and seller agree to such an arrangement.

The interest rate, any discount points and the length of time the lender will honor the loan terms are all freely negotiable. Lenders may agree to offer the loan terms for a definite period of time (a 30, 60 or 90 day lock-in or rate lock), or may refuse to do so. Lenders may require payment of a committment fee for binding themselves into an agreement for a specific period of time, or to make the loan on fixed terms, or to limit the extent to which such terms may change. You will want to ask your lender for a written agreement.

The terms of the agreement with the lender will determine the degree, if any, that the interest rate and discount points may change prior to closing. Any increase in the discount points or an increase of more than 1% in the interest rate requires reprocessing of the loan approval by HUD or the Direct Endorsement lender.

The longer the term of the mortgage, the lower will be the amount of monthly payment, but the higher the total amount of interest paid. For a 20-year $40,000 mortgage at 10%, the monthly payment to principal and interest is $386.40. It is $351.20 for a 30-year mortgage. The total interest over 20 years would be $52,736 — the total interest for a 30-year mortgage would be $86,432. As you can plainly see, by extending your mortgage an additional 10 years, you are greatly increasing the amount of money you will be paying. (We will talk about making extra payments to principal to reduce the amount of interest paid later in this text).

8.3   Discount Points

The rate of interest that lenders charge on mortgages is lower at times than the yield required by investors in the market. For this reason, lenders sometimes discount mortgages — i.e. they charge "points" to make up the difference between the mortgage interest rate and the yield required in the market. A point is equal to one dollar for every hundred dollars of the mortgage amount. The number of points charged varies in different places and times, and among different lenders.

8.4   Monthly Payment

The monthly mortgage payment includes interest, principal (part of the loan balance), amounts for fire and other property insurance, taxes and special assessments, and for certain FHA programs, and mortgage insurance premiums.

Monthly Payment for Principal and Interest on a 30-Year Fixed Rate, Level Payment Mortgage

Mortgage Amount	Interest Rate				
	9.0%	9.5%	10.0%	10.5%	11.0%
$30,000	$241.50	$252.30	$263.40	$274.50	$285.90
$40,000	$322.00	$336.40	$351.20	$366.00	$381.20
$50,000	$402.50	$420.50	$439.00	$457.50	$476.50
$60,000	$483.00	$504.00	$526.80	$549.00	$571.80
$70,000	$563.50	$58.70	$614.60	$640.50	$667.10

Typically, the combined monthly payment for principal, interest, taxes and insurance should be no more than 28 or 29 percent of your total monthly income.

Equal Opportunity in Housing

Racial discrimination in housing of any size is a violation of the Civil Rights Act of 1866. In addition, the Civil Rights Act of 1968 contains a Federal Fair Housing Law (Title VIII) which established fair housing as the policy of the United States. This law prohibits discrimination on the basis of race, color, religion, sex and national origin.

Persons complaining of discrimination in housing have a choice of remedies, including filing a civil action in Federal court (or in some cases, state courts), or complaining to HUD's Office of Fair Housing and Equal Opportunity.

8.5 Section 203(b) — Home Mortgage Insurance [Federal Domestic Assistance Codes 14.117 And 14.118]

Section 203(b) of the National Housing Act provides a program of mortgage insurance to assist homebuyers in the purchase of new and existing one-to-four-family dwellings. It is the basic and most commonly used HUD program. This program is available for use in all areas, both rural and urban, provided a market exists for the property and it meets HUD's Minimum Property Standards.

Mortgage Limits

	Standard Limit	High Cost Areas* up to
Single-family homes	$ 67,500	$101,250
Two-family homes	76,000	114,000
Three-family homes	92,000	138,000
Four-family homes	107,000	160,500

* Certain areas are eligible for larger mortgage amounts because of the high cost of housing. Information about a particular area's mortgage limit may be obtained at local HUD Field Offices or approved lending institutions.

Ratio of Loan to Property Value

If the purchaser intends to live in the home, the amount of a Section 203(b) loan may be up to 97 percent of the first $25,000 plus 95 percent of the remainder, based on HUD's or VA's appraised value of the property plus closing costs. If the property is valued at $50,000 or less, the mortgage can be 97 percent of value.

Special terms are available for qualified veterans purchasing single-family homes. The veteran must get a Certificate of Eligibility from the Veterans Administration (VA) to obtain these special terms. Qualifications are less stringent than those for eligibility under the VA home loan programs, and there is no limit on the number of times an eligible veteran can use his/her eligibility in HUD programs.

If the mortgage covers a dwelling appraised for mortgage insurance after building begins and before the house is a year old, the mortgage limit is 90 percent of value.

If the owner is refinancing an existing mortgage, the HUD-insured mortgage can be no more than the greater of the following:

- 85 percent of the appraised value plus closing costs; or

- the sum of the unpaid balance of the old mortgage and the costs for any repairs or improvements and for obtaining the loan.

If the home is being bought or built as an investment, the loan is limited to 75 percent of value.

Downpayment

The downpayment is the difference between the insured mortgage and the amount it costs to acquire the home. The total cost, called the "acquisition cost", includes the purchase price plus closing costs to be paid by the purchaser. The acquisition cost does not include prepaid items or non-realty items such as furniture.

The maximum mortgage amount which HUD will insure is figured on whichever is less:

- the HUD or VA estimate of the value of the property plus closing costs; or

- the acquisition cost.

The downpayment (including closing costs to be paid by the borrower) and the prepaid items must be paid in cash or its equivalent.

A buyer 60 years of age or older may borrow the money for downpayment and prepaid items from a person or corporation approved by HUD. Other buyers may borrow money for the down payment, but the loan must be secured by real marketable assets other than the property being purchased.

Time Allowed for Repayment of Mortgage (Mortgage Term)

A Section 203(b) mortgage may be repaid in monthly payments over a term of 10, 20, 25, or 30 years. In a few special cases the term may be 35 years.

Typical Transactions

The following table shows, for homes of various values, the highest mortgage amount that can be insured under Section 203(b), and the smallest downpayments (not including the MIP).

Proposed and Existing Construction
Owner-Occupant 1-Family Homes

FHA Appraised Value & Closing Costs	Maximum Mortgage Amount	Minimum Required Investment (excluding MIP)
$ 30,000	$29,100	$ 900
40,000	38,800	1,200
50,000	48,500	1,500
60,000	57,500	2,500
70,000	67,000	3,000

For every $1,000 more in value above $50,000 an additional $50 must be paid in cash. For example, a home appraised at $71,000 requires $3,050 down. Mortgage amounts may be increased and cash payments reduced for qualified veterans. The minimum required investment is somewhat higher for existing construction under one year old.

8.6   **Section 245(a) — Graduated Payment Mortgage (GPM) [Federal Domestic Assistance Code 14.159]**

Lower Initial Mortgage Payments

The GPM program is a variation of the regular HUD/FHA mortgage insurance program. It can allow the purchase of a home with a reasonable downpayment and lower initial monthly payments in the early years of the loan.

With a GPM, mortgage payments rise gradually for a set period of years, then level off and remain steady for the balance of the mortgage. In other words, a GPM enables borrowers to tailor their monthly payments to meet rising income.

How GPM Works

Under the GPM program the homebuyer will, in effect, be borrowing additional money during the early years of the mortgage which will be used to reduce the monthly payments. The additional loan is added to the outstanding mortgage payments in later years.

Five Plans

There are five basic GPM plans which vary the rate of monthly payment increases (from 2 to 7½ percent) and the number of years over which the payments increase (5 or 10 years). The greater the rate of increase, or the longer the period of increase, the lower the mortgage payments are in the early years. After a period of 5 or 10 years, depending on which plan is selected, the mortgage payments level off and stay at that level for the remainder of the loan. GPM payments increase each *year*, not each month.

Plan I   Monthly mortgage payments increase 2½ percent each year for five years.

Plan II   Monthly mortgage payments increase 5 percent each year for five years.

Plan III   Monthly mortgage payments increase 7½ percent each year for five years.

Plan IV   Monthly mortgage payments increase 2 percent each year for ten years.

Plan V   Monthly mortgage payments increase 3 percent each year for ten years.

Mortgage Limits

The GPM program is limited to owner-occupants. The principal amount of the mortgage cannot exceed the *lesser* of:

- 97 percent of the first $25,000 of value and closing costs, plus 95 percent of the remainder, up to $67,500 (or up to $101,250 in designated high cost areas); or

- an amount which, when added to all deferred interest under the financing plan selected, will not exceed 97 percent of the appraised value of the property. If the borrower is a veteran, the mortgage amount, when added to all deferred interest, cannot exceed the applicable limit for veterans under Section 203(b).

Downpayment

The minimum cash investment will be the greater of:

- 3 percent of the first $25,000 plus 5 percent of the remainder; or

- that amount necessary to cover the difference between the maximum insurable loan amount and the acquisition cost.

Mortgage Term: Same as Section 203(b).

Sample

To give you an idea of how a GPM works, the table below compares the payment schedule of an ordinary FHA-insured loan with the most frequently used of the five GPM plans. Under the GPM plan shown, mortgage payments would increase 7½ percent each year for five years before leveling off.

Assume: Mortgage Amount = $50,000
Interest Rate   = 12 percent
Term   = 30 years
                         (360 payments)

Mortgage Payment Each Month:

Year	Regular HUD/FHA Insured Loan	GPM Loan
1	$ 495.50	$ 379.80
2	495.50	408.29
3	495.50	438.91
4	495.50	471.82
5	495.50	507.21
6	495.50	545.25
7	495.50	545.25
Remaining Payments	495.50	545.25

8.7 Section 245(a) Growing Equity Mortgage (GEM)

A GEM is a type of graduated payment mortgage and is eligible for mortgage insurance under 245(a). Unlike a GPM, there is no interest deferral or negative amortization associated with a GEM. Scheduled increases in monthly payments are applied directly to principal reduction. As a result, GEMs have substantially shorter mortgage terms than typical GPM or level payment mortgages. This shorter term dramatically reduces the total cost of the mortgage to the mortgagor.

Mortgage Limit: Same as Section 203(b).

Loan-to-Value Ratio: Same as Section 203(b).

Downpayment: Since there is no negative amortization on these loans, the downpayment on GEMs is the same as required under Section 203(b).

8.8 Section 221(d)(2) — Home Mortgage Insurance for Low and Moderate Income Families [Federal Domestic Assistance Code 14.120]

Section 221(d)(2) provides mortgage insurance for loans used to finance the purchase of low cost one-to-four family for low or moderate income families, or families displaced by governmental action (urban renewal, code enforcement, condemnation, etc.), or displaced as a result of a disaster declared by the President to be a major disaster.

Mortgage Limits

	Standard Limits	High-Cost Areas
		Up to
1 family	$31,000	$36,000
1 family (5 or more persons)	$36,000	$42,500
2 family	$35,000	$45,000
3 family	$48,600	$57,600
4 family	$59,400	$68,400

The limits for high-cost areas shown above are available only in those areas in which construction costs are such that suitable housing cannot be constructed within the standard limits. This determination is made by HUD, and limits are established separtely for each area.

8.9   Section 222 — Morgage Insurance for Service Members [Federal Domestic Assistance Code 14.166]

Section 222 provides mortgage insurance for loans financing the purchase of a one-family dwelling or condominium unit by service members on active duty in the Coast Guard or National Oceanic and Atmospheric Administration. The Department of Defense has suspended its future participation in this program. The mortgage insurance premium is paid directly to HUD by the employing agency during the period of the borrower's active service.

9.0 HERE ARE THE STEPS YOU NEED TO TAKE TO FIND OUT ABOUT TAX-DELINQUENT PROPERTIES IN YOUR AREA

First, open the phone book to COUNTY GOVERNMENT. Look under COUNTY TAX COLLECTOR, COUNTY TAX ASSESSOR, COUNTY TREASURER, PROPERTY REDEMPTION, or some such similar department title.

Call each of these offices and tell them you want information about tax-delinquent property for sale. Each area handles this in their own way. Some hold a sale every other month, some have a sale every other year, some sell properties as they become available. Remember, you will have to ask *specific* questions to get the answers you need. Have a pen and paper ready to take notes and phone numbers. Ask:

"When homeowners are delinquent in paying their property taxes and they don't pay within an allotted time, when and how do you go about selling the properties?"

After they tell you, ask:

"Do you have any properties now?" and **"How and when do you advertise the sale of the properties?"**

They may have an immediate answer for you, but they may tell you that they list through individual brokers. If this is the case, ask them *which ones*, write down names, then CALL THE BROKERS. Sometimes it takes a little perseverance, but you *will* get the information that can lead you to your bargain home!

Also ask if they have a mailing list. If they do, give them your name and address so you will be notified of upcoming sales. You will then receive a list of properties which will be offered at the auction along with legal descriptions of the parcels, assessed value, and minimum opening bid. You may see a street address, but often you will have to dig it out of the legal description (more on this in a minute).

74

If they don't maintain a mailing list, they may tell you to watch the newspaper for announcements of the upcoming sales and they will tell you on which dates to expect to see the notice. In this case, you should put a note on your calendar to remind yourself to start looking more carefully through the newspaper when the time comes.

Some counties may not have tax delinquent sales. They may just not do anything about the delinquent property unless someone comes up to them and says they are interested in buying a property which is delinquent. If this is the case in your area, you can find out which properties are delinquent by *going to the County Courthouse and asking to see the deeds of properties which are delinquent.*

A little note here about the legal descriptions you are going to be seeing. They may say something like "South 0°46'3" east along the Westerly line of said tract, 1817.02 feet; thence North 64°19'7" East ..." This looks a little confusing, but ask a clerk at the COUNTY RECORDS OFFICE to show you the PLAT BOOK and explain how to look up the legal descriptions. After you look up a few, you will get a general idea of a property's location by understanding how the grid pattern is laid out in your area.

Another idea is to check with one of your local title insurance companies, who usually maintain a customer service department; they may be able to simply give you a street address of a property for which you have provided them the parcel number (which appears with the property description, on deeds, etc.).

ONCE YOU HAVE FOUND SOME PROPERTIES WHICH SOUND GOOD TO YOU, you should then go out and personally inspect them. One thing to be aware of is that these properties are sold far below market value, but they are also sold with no guarantees about the condition, the zoning, the title or anything else. To take advantage of the fantastic prices, you have to do a little homework and check out these things before putting your money down at the auction. It's not hard, and the people at the County Records Office will be very helpful and show you where to find out about these details. While you are doing your research, just remember how well-paid you will be for the time you spend once you make a successful purchase and save many thousands of dollars by doing so.

As you are checking, you want to find out if there are any TAX LIENS on the property. The ideal is to find one free and clear of any tax liens, but if there are small amounts due you may decide that those bills could be paid and the property would still be a bargain.

If the property is in a good location for you and you feel you might like to buy it, you should check with the Tax Assessor's Office and find out how much comparable properties have been selling for recently. That will give you a good idea of the market value.

You then ESTABLISH A MAXIMUM BID PRICE in your mind. Make a pact with yourself that you won't go beyond that limit you set for yourself. You have, in a calm frame of mind, decided that a certain price would mean that property would really be a good buy for you, so you don't want to pay too much in the excitement of the auction and get carried away.

Once you have established this maximum price in mind, it is a good idea to **try contacting the owner of the property BEFORE THE AUCTION** and see if you can't come to some agreement. He may say no, but on the other hand, he may be anxious to get it taken care of as soon as possible. You then have the advantage of getting in there before any competition shows up.

AT THE AUCTION, if you don't manage to make a purchase prior to that day, you may or may not have other people who are bidding against you on a particular piece of property. You will have to take with you the full amount in either *cash or certified check* made out for the maximum amount you are going to bid. (If you win with a lesser bid, they will give you a refund). The opening bid is usually either a set percentage of the value of the property (in some places here in California, it is 25% of value) OR an amount which would cover the fees involved in the sale. If you happen to be the only person interested in that property, you will only have to offer the minimum bid and it is yours!

9.1   Some Examples

Just to give you an idea of how things are handled differently in each area, I called around several counties surrounding Santa Barbara, California. Los Angeles County holds a sale every year or every other year in February. They prepare a list of properties in November, so you have that much time to check them out. They charge $10 for the list of properties and at the last sale they had 815 properties, of which about 30 were houses. The clerk did say that the houses often get redeemed before going up for auction since a tax sale in California dissolves all liens on the property except IRS and other tax liens. That means a bank holding the mortgage would probably pay off the taxes and try to sell the house for at least the amount they were owed on the mortgage plus the back taxes rather than get nothing. There are cases, however, of a house having been owned completely free and clear and the taxes just never were paid until it winds up at the auction.

Kern County holds a tax-delinquent property sale three times a year and offers about 200 properties each time. They maintain a mailing list and offer the properties for an opening bid which is a fraction of the actual value.

San Luis Obispo County has a sale in March of each year and puts the list of properties, assessed value and minimum opening bid required. They usually have 40-50 properties offered in their sale. Generally the opening bid will be 25% of assessed value. The clerk said assessed value tends to be lower than actual market value, so 25% of that can be a very low price indeed!

A lot of the property sold at delinquent tax auctions is vacant land, so it is a good idea for you to study the path of development in the area where the land is. You can tell if new stores and houses are collecting more in one end of town than another, then you just need to look at the land and try to determine how long it would be before the development came right across your piece of land. Since the prices are such bargains, you will find you can afford to buy a piece of vacant land and just hold it while development goes on around you. If you are full of ideas, you might be able to interest a developer in your piece of land. Never forget, lots of people laughed when their friends bought land with nothing but sand and cactus 30 years ago in California, and today that land is Palm Springs — one of the most glamorous resort areas in the world. You must keep an open mind and a sharp eye out!

10.0 <u>INTERNAL REVENUE SERVICE SALES AND AUCTIONS</u>

When Uncle Sam decides to take property from individuals who have failed to honestly report their income to the IRS, what becomes of this bounty? Much of it is sold or auctioned off.

IRS sales and auctions must follow the same regulations nationwide, per Section 6337 and 6339C.

Real estate must be disposed of within 45 days of the seizure, and not less than 10 days from public notice of the sale (such as a newspaper ad).

All real estate has a six-month redemption period; in other words, the original owner or interested party with a claim has the right to purchase the property back by paying the amount sold for plus a 20% prorated interest to the purchaser. (This means that you are at some risk when buying IRS confiscated property with regard to being able to hold on to same).

If your bid buys the property, you receive a tax receipt after 6 months, which you turn in for a tax deed. Here is a second drawback — this is not a guaranteed deed — if someone has a legal claim to the property prior to the IRS, then you stand the chance of losing the property to the original claimant. The IRS does have a title search done prior to the sale, but these are not always foolproof.

You will be required to have a set amount guaranteed, such as a cashiers check, to be allowed into an auction for a property. No item can sell for less than what is owed to the IRS.

Property other than real estate is on a cash-and-carry basis, and is not subject to the six-month redemption period. If the original owner wants an item back, he or she must work out a price that the new owner agrees to — and only if the new owner agrees can the property revert back to the original owner.

Most real estate property goes as follows: a certain amount is guaranteed (usually the amount owed to the IRS, if possible), and if your bid is accepted you pay 25% down and the remainder the next day.

The IRS is divided into 7 regions, with each region divided into district, and each district into various offices.

Each office handles its own sales and is not required to inform any other office or consult them. You will want to watch major newspapers for one of two types of listings: Auction Notices and Classifieds.

You can obtain additional information directly from the IRS by sending a letter to them stating where you are interested in buying property. You can submit this letter to all of the offices listed on the following pages, or submit it only to those areas of interest to you. Within the letter you need to give them your name, address, and type of property you are interested in buying. Send your letters to the appropriate address to the attention of SPECIAL PROCEDURES.

CENTRAL REGION
550 Main Street, Room 7112
Cincinnati, OH 45202
513/684-3612

District Offices:

550 Main Street, Room 5106
Cincinnati, OH

1240 East 9th Street
Cleveland, OH 44199

477 Michigan Ave., Room 2483
Detroit, MI 48226

575 N. Pennsylvania Street
Indianapolis, IN 46204

601 W. Broadway, Room 23
Louisville, KY 40202

425 Juliana Street
Parkersburg, WV 26101

MID-ATLANTIC REGION
841 Chestnut Street, 2nd Floor
Philadelphia, PA 19107
215/597-2040

District Offices:

31 Hopkins Plaza
Baltimore, MD 21201

970 Broad Street
Newark, NJ 07102

600 Arch Street
Federal Offices Building
Philadelphia, PA 19106

1000 Liberty Avenue
Pittsburg, PA 15222

400 North 8th Streeet
Richmond, VA 23240

9th and King Streets
Wilmington, DE 19801

MID-WEST REGION
1 North Wacker Drive
10th Floor
Chicago, IL 60606
312/435-1040

District Offices:

1225 Corporate Boulevard
Aurora, IL 60504

131 East 4th Street
Davenport, IA 52801

7601 South Kostner
South Chicago, IL 60652

7301 North Lincoln Avenue
Lincolnwood, IL 60646

33 East 22nd
Lombard, IL 60148

211 South Court
Rockford, IL 61101

175 East Hawthorne Parkway
Woodland Hills, IL 60001

600 Quail Ridge Road
Westmont, IL 60559

NORTH ATLANTIC REGION
90 Church Street
New York, NY 10007
212/264-7061

District Offices:

Clinton Avenue & N. Pearl Street
Albany, NY 12207

68 Sewall Street
August, ME 04330

JFK Federal Building
Boston, MA 02203

35 Tillary Street
Brooklyn, NY 11202

Thaddeus & Dulsk Fed Office Bldg
111 West Huron Street
Buffalo, NY 14202

Courthouse Plaza
199 Main Street
Burlington, VT 05402

William R. Cotter Federal Bldg.
135 High Street
Hartford, CT 06103

120 Church Street
New York, NY 10007

Federal Building
80 Daniel Street
Portsmouth, NH 03801

380 Westminster Mall
Providence, RI 02903

310 Lowell Street
Andover, MA 01810

1020 Waverly Avenue
Holtsville NY 11799

SOUTHEAST REGION
401 W. Peachtree Street NW
Atlanta, GA 31365
404/331-6048

District Offices:

401 W. Peachtree Street NW
Room 1531
Stop 205-D
Atlanta, GA 30365

500 22nd Street
Birmingham, AL 35233

1835 Assembly Street
Room 408 MDP-14
Columbia, SC 29201

P.O. Box 292590
Stop 6020
Ft. Lauderdale, FL 33329-2590

320 Federal Place
Greensboro, NC 27401

100 W. Capital Street
Suite 504
Jackson, MS 39269

P.O. Box 35045
Jacksonville, FL 32202

70 West Capitol
Stop 34
Little Rock, AR 72203

P.O. Box 1107
Stop 37
Nashville, TN 37202

501 Magazine Street
Stop 9
New Orleans, LA 70130

SOUTHWEST REGION
4050 Alpha Road
12th Floor
Dallas, TX 75244-4203
214/308-7000

District Offices:

517 Gold Avenue SW
Albuquerque, NM 87102

300 East 8th
Austin, TX 78701

308 West 21st Street
Cheyenne, WY 82001

1100 Commerce Street
Dallas, TX 75242

600 17th Street
Denver, CO 80202-2490

322 Briar Park
Houston, TX 77042

P.O. Box 66
200 N.W. 4th, Room 1431
Oklahoma City, OK 73103

212 N. Central Avenue
Room 120
Phoenix, AZ 85004

465 S. 400 East Street
Salt Lake, UT 84111

412 S. Main
Wichita, KS 67202

WESTERN REGION
1650 Mission Street
Room 511
San Francisco, CA 94103
413/556-3300

District Offices:

949 East 36th Avenue
Anchorage, AK 99508

550 W. Fort Street
Boise, ID 83724

PJKK Federal building
300 Ala Moana
Honolulu, HI 96850

2400 Ivila Road
Laguna Niguel, CA 92677

4750 W. Oakey Boulevard
Las Vegas, NV 89102

300 N. Los Angeles Street
Los Angeles, CA 90012

1220 SW 3rd Avenue
Portland, OR 97204

4330 Watt Avenue
North Highland, CA 95660

450 Golden Gate Avenue
SF-4-0-37
San Francisco, CA 94102

55 South Market Street
San Jose, CA 95113

915 2nd Avenue
Seattle, WA 98174

Department of the Treasury/Internal Revenue Service

Notice of **PUBLIC AUCTION SALE**

Under the authority in Internal Revenue Code section 6331, the property described below has been seized for nonpayment of internal revenue taxes due from:

OZZIE & HARRIET SMITH, 123 NOWHERE PL., DAYTON OH

The property will be sold at public auction as provided by Internal Revenue Code section 6355 and related regulations.

Date of Sale: AUGUST 16TH, 1990

Time of Sale: 10:00 AM

Place of Sale: Internal Revenue Svc, Algonquin Rd., Schaumburg, IL

Title Offered: Only the right, title, and interest of OZZIE & HARRIET SMITH in and to the property will be offered for sale. if requested, the Internal Revenue Service will furnish information about possible encumbrances, which may be useful in determining the value of the interest being sold. (See the back of this form for further details.)

Description of Property: All right, title, and interest of Ozzie and Harriet Smith in the beneficial interest and power of direction in Land Trust No. 67219, the trustee of which is American National Bank and Trust Company of Chicago, 33 North LaSalle Street, Chicago, Illinois 60690, and the corpus of which is legally described as follows:

Lot 51 in Arthur T. McIntosh and company's Golf Meadows, a subdivision of part of Section 16, Township 42 North, Range 10, East of the third Principal Merician, According to the Plat thereof Recorded November 20, 1969 as Document Number 21018639, in Cook County, illinois. And commonly known as 1221 Aberdeen, Inverness, Illinois 60067.

Property is a two story custom built 8 year old single family house, consisting of 10 rooms, 3 car garage on over an acre lot.

Property may be Inspected at: 1221 ABERDEEN ROAD, INVERNESS, ILLINOIS

Payment Terms: Deferred payment as follows: 25% upon acceptance of highest bid, balance by 4:00 PM August 17th 1990. Proof of at least $14,000.00 required prior to sale in order to bid.

Form of Payment: All payments must be by cash, certified check, cashier's or treasurer's check or by a United States postal, bank, express, or telegraph money order. Make check or money order payable to the Internal Revenue Service.

84

Nature of Title: The right, title, and interest of the taxpayer (named on the front of this form) in and to the property is offered for sale subject to any prior valid outstanding mortgages, encumbrances, or other liens in favor of third parties against the taxpayer that are superior to the len of the United States. All property is offered for sale "where is" and "as is" and without recourse against the United States. No guaranty or warranty, express or implied, is made as to the validity of the title, quality, quantity, weight, size, or condition of any of the property, or its fitness for any use or purpose. No claim will be considered for allowance or adjustment or for rescission of the sale based on failure of the property to conform with any expressed or implied representation.

Redemption Rights The rights of redemption, as specified in Internal Revenue Code section 6337, are quoted as follows:

Sec. 6337. Redemption of Property.

(a) Before Sale. — Any person whose property has been levied upn shall have the right to pay the amount due together with the expenses of the proceeding, if any, to the Secretary at any time prior to the sale thereof, and upon such payment the Secretary shall restore such property to him, and all further proceedings in connection with the levy on such property shall cease from the time of such payment.

(b) Redemption of Real Estate After Sale.

(1) Period. — The owners of any real property sold as provided in section 6335, their heirs, executors, or administrators, or any person having any interest therein, or a lien thereon, or any person in their behalf, shall be permitted to redeem the property sold, or any particular tract of such property at any time within 180 days after the sale thereof.

(2) Price. — Such property or tract of property shall be permitted to be redeemed upon payment to the purchaser, or in case he cannot be found in the county in which the property to be redeemed is situated, then to the Secretary, for the use of the purchaser, his heirs, or assigns, the amount paid by such purchaser and interest thereon at the rate of 20 percent per annum.

Effect of Junior Encum-brances *Sec. 6339(c). Effect of Junior Encumbrances.*
A certificate of sale of personal property given or a deed to real property from
from all liens, encumbrances, and titles over which the lien of the United States with
respect to which the levy was made had priority.

.FORM 2434-B (Rev. Sept. 1985)	Department of the Treasury — Internal Revenue Service	PAGE ONE
	Notice of Encumbrances Against or Interests in Property Offered for Sale	

As of this date, the following are the encumbrances against or interests in the property (as described in the Notice of Public Auction or Notice of Sealed Bid Sale) that was seized for nonpayment of Internal Revenue taxes due from. OZZIE & HARRIET SMITH

Some of these encumbrances or interests may be superior to the lien of the United States.

Type of Encumbrance or Interest	Amount of Encumbrance or Interest	Date of Instrument Creating Encumbrance or Interest	Date and Place Recorded	Name and Address of Party Holding Encumbrance or Interest	Date of Information
Mortgage	198,426.03	02/04/83	RECORDER OF DEEDS COOK COUNTY CHICAGO, ILLINOIS 02/08/83	NORTHBROOK TRUST & SAVINGS P.O. BOX 7129 CHICAGO, ILLINOIS 60680	4/30/90
Mortgage	26,418.78	07/17/87	RECORDER OF DEEDS COOK COUNTY CHICAGO, ILLINOIS 07/30/87	THE FIRST NATIONAL BANK OF CHICAGO ONE 1ST NAT'L PLAZA CHICAGO, IL. 60670	01/12/90
Judgement	0	04/27/84	RECORDER OF DEEDS COOK COUNTY CHICAGO, ILLINOIS 04/27/84	KROHN ENTERPRISES INC. @E.H.KROLLS 55 N. SMITH PALATINE, IL. 60067	06/11/9
FEDERAL TAX LEIN	489,399.19	11/04/88	RECORDER OF DEEDS COOK COUNTY CHICAGO, IL.11/4/88	INTERNAL REVENUE SERVICE 860 ALGONQUIN RD. SCHAUMBURG, IL. 60173	06/18/90
Judgement	1,527.23	11/12/89	RECORDER OF DEEDS COOK COUNTY CHICAGO, ILLINOIS 11/2/89	WCI FINANCIAL CORP. @ JOHN HASENMILLER 343 S. DEARBORN SUITE1010 CHICAGO, IL. 60604	06/11/90
REAL ESTATE	0	01/03/89	RECORDER OF DEEDS COOK COUNTY CHICAGO, IL. 01/03/89	NATIONAL INDEMNITY CORP. 100 N. LASALLE ST. CHICAGO, ILLINOIS	05/21/90
Federal Tax Lein	44,253.56	06/21/90	RECORDER OF DEEDS COOK COUNTY CHICAGO, ILLINOIS 06/27/90	INTERNAL REVENUE SERVICE 860 ALGONQUIN RD. SCHAUMBURG, IL. 60173	06/28/90
			SEE PAGE TWO		

NOTE: The Internal Revenue Service does not warrant the correctness or completeness of the above information, and provides the information solely to help the prospective bidders determine the value of the interest being sold. Bidders should, therefore, verify for themselves the validity, priority, and amount of encumbrances against the property offered for sale. Each party listed above was mailed a notice of sale on or before _7/17/90_ (date)_

Signature	Name and Title (typed)	Date
M. Epperly	M. EPPERLY REVENUE OFFICER	6/19/90

Form 2434-B (Rev. 9-8!

	Department of the Treasury — Internal Revenue Service
Form 2434-B (Rev. Sept. 1985)	Notice of Encumbrances Against or Interests In Property Offered for Sale

Authority and Effect of Sale

Pursuant to authority contained in sections 6331 and 6335 of the Internal Revenue Code and the regulations thereunder, and by virtue of a levy issued by authority of the District Director of Internal Revenue, the right, title, and interest (in the notice of sale) of the taxpaper (whose name appears on the reverse side of this document) will be sold.

Such interest is offered subject to any prior outstanding mortgages, encumbrances, or other liens in favor of third parties, which are valid against the taxpayer and are superior to the lien of the United States. The reverse of this document provides information regarding possible encumbrances or interests which may be useful in determining the value of the interest being sold. All interest of record were mailed a notice of sale.

The property will be sold "as is" and "where is" and without recourse against the United States. The Government makes no guaranty or warranty, expressed or implied, as to the validity of the title, quality, quantity, weight, size, or condition of the property, or its fitness for any use or purpose. No claim will be considered for allowance or adjustment or for rescission of the sale based upon failure of the property to conform with any representation, expressed or implied.

Notice of sale has been given in accordance with legal requirements. If the property is offered by more than one method, all bids will be considered tentative until the highest bid has been determined. The property will be sold to the highest bidder, and the sale will be final upon acceptance of the highest bid in accordance with the terms of the sale.

Payment must be made by cash, certified check, cashier's or treasurer's check or by a United States Postal, bank, express, or telegraph money order. All checks or money orders must be made payable to the Internal Revenue Service. A certificate of sale will be delivered to the successful bidder as soon as possible upon receipt of full payment of the purchase price.

Section 6339(c) of the Code states that a certificate of sale of personal property given or a deed to real property executed pursuant to section 6338 will discharge that property from all liens, encumbrances, and titles which are junior to the federal tax lien by virtue of which the levy was made. If real property is involved, section 6337 of the Code provides that the taxpayer, his or her heirs, executors, or administrators, or any person having an interest therein, or lien thereon, or any person in behalf of the taxpayer may redeem real property within 180 days from the date of its sale by the Internal Revenue Service. The redemption price to be paid to the successful bidder is the successful bib price plus 20 percent per year interest from the date of payment by the successful bidder to the date of redemption. If the property is not redeemed within the 180-day period, the District Director shall, upon receipt of the certificate of sale, issue a deed to the purchaser, or his assignee.

Department of the Treasury/Internal Revenue Service

Notice of **PUBLIC AUCTION SALE**

Under the authority in Internal Revenue Code section 6331, the property described below has been seized for nonpayment of internal revenue taxes due from:

OZZIE & HARRIET SMITH, 123 NOWHERE PL., DAYTON OH

The property will be sold at public sale under sealed bid as provided by Internal Revenue Code section 6335 and related regulations.

Date Bids will be Opened: August 1, 1990

Time Bids will be Opened: 10:00 AM

Place of Sale: Internal Revenue Svc, Kohler Memorial Dr, Sheboygan, WI

Title Offered: Only the right, title, and interest of OZZIE & HARRIET SMITH in and to the property will be offered for sale. If requested, the Internal Revenue Service will furnish information about possible encumbrances, which may be useful in determining the value of the interest being sold. (See "Nature of Title" below for further details.)

Description of Property: Re-sub'd of Crystal Lake Park, Lot 83, BLK 9, also vacated street between said Lot and Lot 47, BLK 8, Section 32, Township 16, Range 21. Two story frame cottage building size 33 x 21 feet. Hot tub and sauna in lower level. The well is shared with four other cottages. Right to use 10 feet of the beach area. Minimum bid — $43,992.44.

Property may be Inspected at: #228 Fire #7406 Crystal Lake Drive, Crystal Lake, WI

Submission of bids: All bids must be submitted on Form 2222, Sealed Bid for purchase of Seized Property. Contact the office indicated below for Forms 2222 and information aqbout the property. Submit bids to the person named below before the time bids will be opened.

Payment Terms: Bids must be accompanied by the full amount of the bid if it totals $200 or less. If the total bid is more than $200, submit 20 percent of the amount bid or $200, whichever is greater. On acceptance of the highest bid, the balance due, if any, will be * Required in ful * Deferred as follows: Balance within one month of sale date.

Form of Payment: All payments must be by cash, certified check, cashier's or treasurer's check or by a United States postal, bank, express, or telegraph money order. Make check or money order payable to the Internal Revenue Service.

88

Nature of Title:	The right, title, and interest of the taxpayer (named above) in and to the property is offered for sale *subject to any prior valid outstanding mortgages, encumbrances, or other liens in favor of third parites against the taxpayer that are superior to thelien of the United States.* All property is offered for sale "where is" and "as is" and without recourse against the United States. No guaranty or warranty, expressed or implied, is made as to the validity of the title, quality, quanity, wight, size, or condition of any of the property, or its fitness for any use or purpose. No claim will be considered for allowance or adjustment or for rescission of the sale based on failure of the property to conform with any expressed or implied representation.
Redemption Rights:	The rights of redemption, as specified in Internal Revenue Code Section property is quoted as follows:

Section 6337. Redemption of Property.

(a) Before Sale. — Any person whose property has been levied upon shall have the right to pay the amount fdue, together with the expenses of the proceeding, if any, to the Secretary at any time prior to the sale thereof, and upon such payment, the Secretary shall resotre such property to him and all further proceedings in connection with the levey on such property shall cease from the time of such payment.

(b) Redemption of Real Estate After Sale.

(1)   Period — The owners of any real property sold as provided in Section 6335, their heirs, executors, or administrators, or any person having any interest therein, or a lien thereon, or any person in their behalf, shall be permitted to redeem the property sold, or any particular tract of such property at any time within 180 days after the sale thereof.

(2)   Price — Such property or tract of property shall be permitted to be redeemed upon payment to the purchaser, or in case he cannot be found in the county in which the property to be redeemed is situated, then to the Secretary, for the use of the purchases, his heirs, or assigns, the amount paid by such purchaser and interest thereon at the rate of 20 percent per annum.

Effect of Junior Encum- brances	*Sec. 6339(c). Effect of Junior Encumbrances.* A certificate of sale of personal property or a deed to real property from all liens, encumbrances, and titles over which the lien of the United States with respect to which the levy was made had priority.

FORM 2434-B (Rev. Sept. 1985)	Department of the Treasury — Internal Revenue Service
	Notice of Encumbrances Against or Interests in Property Offered for Sale

As of this date, the following are the encumbrances against or interests in the property (as described in the Notice of Public Auction or Notice of Sealed Bid Sale) that was seized for nonpayment of Internal Revenue taxes due from: OZZIE & HARRIET SMITH

Some of these encumbrances or interests may be superior to the lien of the United States.

Type of Encumbrance or Interest	Amount of Encumbrance or Interest	Date of Instrument Creating Encumbrance or Interest	Date and Place Recorded	Name and Address of Party Holding Encumbrance or Interest	Date of Information
Mortgage	19,756.56	01/12/90	RECORDER OF DEEDS COOK COUNTY CHICAGO, IL. 07/30/87	THE FIRST NATIONAL BANK OF CHICAGO ONE 1ST NAT'L PLAZA CHICAGO, ILLINOIS 60670	06/18/90

NOTE: The Internal Revenue Service does not warrant the correctness or completeness of the above information, and provides the information solely to help the prospective bidders determine the value of the interest being sold. Bidders should, therefore, verify for themselves the validity, priority, and amount of encumbrances against the property offered for sale. Each party listed above was mailed a notice of sale on or before ___7/17/90___ (date) _M. Epperly_

Signature	Name and Title (typed)	Date
M. Epperly	M. EPPERLY REVENUE OFFICER	06/19/90

Form **2434-B** (Rev. 9 85)

90

| Form 2434-B | Department of the Treasury — Internal Revenue Service |
| (Rev. Sept. 1985) | Notice of Encumbrances Against or Interests in Property Offered for Sale |

Authority and Effect of Sale

Pursuant to authority contained in sections 6331 and 6335 of the Internal Revenue Code and the regulations thereunder, and by virtue of a levy issued by authority of the District Director of Internal Revenue, the right, title, and interest (in the notice of sale) of the taxpaper (whose name appears on the reverse side of this document) will be sold.

Such interest is offered subject to any prior outstanding mortgages, encumbrances, or other liens in favor of third parties, which are valid against the taxpayer and are superior to the lien of the United States. The reverse of this document provides information regarding possible encumbrances or interests which may be useful in determining the value of the interest being sold. All interest of record were mailed a notice of sale.

The property will be sold "as is" and "where is" and without recourse against the United States. The Government makes no guaranty or warranty, expressed or implied, as to the validity of the title, quality, quantity, weight, size, or condition of the property, or its fitness for any use or purpose. No claim will be considered for allowance or adjustment or for rescission of the sale based upon failure of the property to conform with any representation, expressed or implied.

Notice of sale has been given in accordance with legal requirements. If the property is offered by more than one method, all bids will be considered tentative until the highest bid has been determined. The property will be sold to the highest bidder, and the sale will be final upon acceptance of the highest bid in accordance with the terms of the sale.

Payment must be made by cash, certified check, cashier's or treasurer's check or by a United States Postal, bank, express, or telegraph money order. All checks or money orders must be made payable to the Internal Revenue Service. A certificate of sale will be delivered to the successful bidder as soon as possible upon receipt of full payment of the purchase price.

Section 6339(c) of the Code states that a certificate of sale of personal property given or a deed to real property executed pursuant to section 6338 will discharge that property from all liens, encumbrances, and titles which are junior to the federal tax lien by virtue of which the levy was made. If real property is involved, section 6337 of the Code provides that the taxpayer, his or her heirs, executors, or administrators, or any person having an interest therein, or lien thereon, or any person in behalf of the taxpayer may redeem real property within 180 days from the date of its sale by the Internal Revenue Service. The redemption price to be paid to the successful bidder is the successful bib price plus 20 percent per year interest from the date of payment by the successful bidder to the date of redemption. If the property is not redeemed within the 180-day period, the District Director shall, upon receipt of the certificate of sale, issue a deed to the purchaser, or his assignee.

11.0 THE U.S. GENERAL SERVICES ADMINISTRATION FEDERAL PROPERTY RESOURCES SERVICE

The *U.S. Real Property Sales List* is published quarterly by the Federal Property Resources Services (FPRS) of the U.S. General Services Administration (GSA).

Operating under the authority of the Federal Property and Administrative Services Act of 1949, FPRS is a nationwide organization engaged in selling property no longer needed by the Federal Government. FPRS is staffed by real estate professionals and markets property in all 50 states, the District of Columbia, Puerto Rico, the Virgin Islands, and the U.S. Pacific territories.

Properties vary widely in value and type. They may include former Federal office buildings, small parcels of unimproved land, high-rise building sites in large cities, major acreage for commercial or industrial development, and warehouses. Occasionally, former military family housing and individual residences confiscated by law enforcement officials may also be listed.

As a representative of all taxpayers, the GSA is required by law to obtain fair market value for any property it sells. Generally, major properties are sold at auction, and less expensive properties are disposed of by sealed bid. In any case, bidders are required to place a bid deposit. Sealed bids are made on a special bidding form. The bids are opened on a specific date, and the property is awarded to the highest bidder at or above fair market value.

FPRS has four regional sales offices. Therefore, the *U.S. Real Property Sales List* is divided into four sections with sales properties listed by state and city or county. A map shows the states covered by each regional office; FPRS also has two field offices and some of the listings ask you to contact these offices. If you desire additional information about property being offered or about the real property sales program, simply write or phone one of the regional or field offices. Addresses and telephone numbers are provided on the following pages.

Sample order forms are provided on pages 88 and 89. You may wish to make copies so you can request notices of future sales of individual properties.

Boston Real Estate Sales Office
(617) 565-5700

ILLINOIS

Forest Park
Parcel, 14 acres of land improved with seven single-family houses and tennis courts, adjoining Forest Park Mall shopping center near Des Plaines Avenue, south of Roosevelt Road in Chicago, Suburban-commercial. Auction.
Call (312) 353-6045 for sale date.

MASSACHUSETTS

Granby
Portion, former Westover Communication Transmit Facility, approximately 100 acres, located off Green Meadow Road. Rural-residential. Auction. July 24, 1990.

MINNESOTA

Minneapolis
Portion, Fort Snelling, 11.02 acres improved with seven storage buildings near Minneapolis International Airport and expressway. Commercial. Auction. Call (312) 353-6045 for sale date.

PUERTO RICO

San Juan
Residencia Universitaria Vedruna at Gandara Avenue — Corner #3, Capetillo Road, structural shell of a two-story building of 22,000 square feet on approximately 0.33 of an acre. Urban-light industrial/commercial/residential. Sealed bid. August 28, 1990

WISCONSIN

Kaukauna
Retail/office building, 9,000 square feet on 0.3 of an acre, 112 Main Avenue. Urban. Auction. Call (312) 353-6045

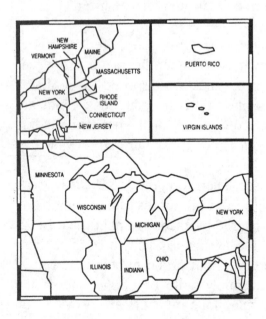

Atlanta Real Estate Sales Office
(404) 331-5133

NORTH CAROLINA

Wake Forest
U.S. Post Office Building, one story with basement, 7,846 square feet on 0.41 of an acre. Auction. Call sales office for date.

PENNSYLVANIA

Johnstown
Hahn Building, three story brick and concrete block structure, 36,907 square feet on approximately 0.75 of an acre. Light industrial. Auction. July 17, 1990.

Johnstown
McLaughlin Tire Center, three story brick structure, 26,964 square feet with a steel garage addition on approximately 0.63 of an acre. Auction. July 17, 1990.

Pittsburgh
Office building, four story brick structure. 62,500 square feet on 0.8 of an acre. Auction. July 17, 1990.

Phoenixville
Portion. Former Valley Forge General Hospital, approximately one acre improved with two concrete reservoirs. Possible residential. Auction. July 26, 1990.

SOUTH CAROLINA

Beech Island
Parcel, 6.55 acres improved with a two-story, three-bedroom, one and one-half baths, 1,826 square-foot residence. Auction. August 23, 1990.

Charleston
Boatyard, 10 acres improved with several repair sheds. Auction. August 21, 1990.

Charleston
Deep water marine facility, 10.5 acres improved with two ware houses and a shop building. Auction. Call sales office for date.

Hilton Head
Residence, one story, three bedrooms, two baths, waterfront on two sides. Auction. August 23, 1990.

WEST VIRGINIA

Petersburg
Single family residence, four bedrooms, one and one-half baths, garage, 3,204 square feet on 0.2 of an acre. Auction. July 12, 1990.

Fort Worth Real Estate Sale Office
(817) 334-2331

KANSAS

Sedgwick and Reno Counties
Portion, Cheney Dan and Reservoir project, eight contiguous parcels totaling 150.8 acres. Rural-residential/agricultural. Auction. Call sales office for date.

LOUISIANA

Union Parish
Portion, Old Lock and Dam No. 5 project, 13.5 acres of unimproved land across the Quachita River from Sterlington. Residential/commercial/agricultural. Sealed bid. August 9, 1990.

Berwick
Former MSO Morgan City Housing Property, 40 acres of unimproved land, adjacent to Berwick High School. Residential. Sealed bid. July 26, 1990.

MISSOURI

Bates, Henry, and St. Clair Counties
Portion, Harry S. Truman Dam and Reservoir project, 178.41 acres in four contiguous tract of unimproved land. Residential/agricultural. Sealed bid. Call sales office for date.

NEW MEXICO

McKinley County
Fort Wingate Trading Post, 16.92 acres improved with one building on Highway 400 approximately 3 mile south of I-40. Commercial/residential. Call sales office for date.

Socarro County
Portion, Magdalena Indian School, 8.78 acres improved with 14 buildings including house, apartments and dormitory buildings. Residential/commercial. Sealed bid. Call sales office for date.

NORTH DAKOTA

Jamestown
Former U.S. Post Office Building, 23,100 square feet, on 0.42 of an acre, 222 1st Avenue South. Commercial. Sealed bid. August 2, 1990.

OKLAHOMA

Pontotoc County
Parcel, 2.81 acres improved with small concrete block building. Residential/agricultural/commercial. Sealed bid. July 19, 1990.

Marshall and Love Counties
Portions, Denison Dam-Lake Texoma project, 16 noncontiguous parcels totaling 495.5 acres of unimproved land. Agricultural/recreational. Auction. July 27, 1990.

SOUTH DAKOTA

Butte County
Former Newell Agricultural Experiment Station, 360 acres with improvements (houses, barns, irrigation system, etc). Auction. August 22, 1990.

TEXAS

Caldwell
Former U.S. Post Office Building, one and one-half stories, 4,635 square feet, on 0.69 of an acre, 102 West Fox Street. Commercial. Auction. July 20, 1990.

Denton County
Portion, Lewisville Lake project, 1.5 acres of unimproved land. Agricultural/rural-residential. Sealed bid. July 26, 1990.

Houston
Portion, Lyndon B. Johnson NASA facility, 37 acres of unimproved land on Space Center Boulevard. Commercial. Sealed bid. August 2, 1990.

UTAH

Wendover
Parcel, 0.54 acres of unimproved land. Residential. Sealed bid. Call sales office for date.

San Francisco Real Estate Sales Office
(415) 744-5952

ALASKA

Fairbanks
Portion, Fort Wainwright family housing annex, 1.9 acres of unimproved land adjacent to Federal building, Commercial. Sealed bid. August 21, 1990. Call (415) 744-5937 for more information.

CALIFORNIA

San Diego
Portion, Miramar Navel Air Station, about 47 acres unimproved fronts on Claremont Mesa Boulevard, east of I-15, west of Santo Road and south of State Route 52. Manufacturing/industrial/commercial. Auction. August 4, 1990. Call (415) 744-5959 for more information.

OREGON

Astoria
Portion, Tonque Point Job Corps Center, approximately 22.77 acres of unimproved land located 2 mile east of Astoria. Sealed bid. August 7, 1990. Call (415) 744-5947 for more information.

WASHINGTON

Benton County
Twenty houses for off-site removal. 17 two-bedroom, one-bath, 1,334 square-foot ramblers and 3 three-bedroom, one-bath ramblers. Auction. Call sales office for date.

Clark County
Residence, three bedrooms, three baths, 1,980 square feet, 40 by 60 foot metal barn on 21 acres. 5 acre zoning. North of Vancouver. Rural/residential. Sealed bid. Call sales office for date.

King County
Seven parcels of unimproved land ranging from 5.3 to 26.8 acres, all subject to overhead powerline easements. No structures permitted. Rural-agricultural. Sealed bid. September 26, 1990. Call (206) 931-7547 for more information.

King County
Residence, three bedrooms, one and three-quarters baths, 1,980 square feet, with two-car garage, located on a cul-de-sac. Federal Way area. Auction. Call sales office for date.

King County
Residence, three bedrooms, one and one-half baths, one-car garage, near Seattle-Tacoma International Airport. Auction. Call sales office for date.

Thurston County
Residence, older home on 8 acres of land, south of Olympia. Sealed bid. Call sales office for date.

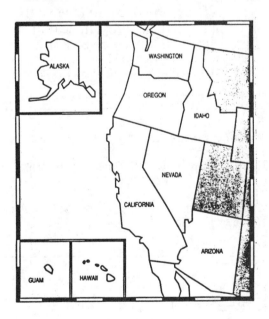

Real Estate Sales Offices

FPRS has regional real estate offices in Boston, MA; Atlanta, GA; Ft. Worth, TX; and San Francisco, CA. Field offices are located in Chicago, IL, and Auburn, WA. The addresses and telephone numbers are as follows:

REGIONAL OFFICES

Office of Real Estate Sales (2DR-1)
U.S. General Services Administration
10 Causeway Street
Boston, MA 02222
(617) 565-5700

Office of Real Estate Sales (4DR)
U.S. General Services Administration
75 Spring Street, Room 818
Atlanta, GA 30303
(404) 331-5133

Office of Real Estate Sales (7DR)
U.S. General Services Administration
819 Taylor Street, Room 11A26
Ft. Worth, TX 76102
(817) 334-2331

Office of Real Estate (9DR)
U.S. General Services Administration
525 Market Street
San Francisco, CA 94105
(415) 744-5952

FIELD OFFICES

Office of Real Estate Sales (2DRF-5)
U.S. General Services Administration
230 South Dearborn Street, Room 3316
Chicago, IL 60604
(312) 353-6045

Office of Real Estate Sales (9DR-F)
U.S. General Services Administration
GSA Center, Room 2476
Auburn, WA 98001
(206) 931-7547

How to Obtain Issues of the U.S. Real Property Sales List

GSA does not maintain a mailing list for future issues of the *U.S. Real Property Sales List.*

If you would like to receive the next edition, complete this order blank and mail it to the address indicated. You will need to send in the order blank from each issue you receive in order to receive the following issue.

Please use correct postage.

— —

Issues of the U.S. Real Property Sales List

Mail to: Properties — C, Consumer Information Center
                    Pueblo, CO 81009

Please send the next issue of the **U.S. Real Property Sales List** to
(type or print in ink):

_____

NAME

_____

STREET

_____

CITY   STATE (TWO-LETTER MAIL CODE)   ZIP

How to Obtain Notices of Individual Sales

If you would like to receive notices of individual sales of U.S. Government real property, complete this form and detach and mail it to us. Your name will be placed on a permanent mailing list for the locations you indicate. Unlike the one above, you need to complete this form only once. Your name address will remain on the list until such time as we ask you to validate the information.

For the **Location** section of the card, you may select up to three states or territories. Write the four-digit numbers of the locations (from the list below) into the boxes. Please print clearly.

0001-AL	0019-IA	0033-NH	0048-TX
0002-AK	0020-KS	0034-NJ	0049-UT
0004-AZ	0021-KY	0035-NM	0050-VT
0005-AR	0022-LA	0036-NY	0051-VA
0006-CA	0023-ME	0037-NC	0053-WA
0008-CO	0024-MD	0038-ND	0054-WV
0009-CT	0025-MA	0039-OH	0055-WI
0010-DE	0026-MI	0040-OK	0056-WY
0012-FL	0027-MN	0041-OR	0057-Am. Samoa
0013-GA	0028-MS	0042-PA	0011-DC
0015-HI	0029-M0	0044-RI	0058-Guam
0016-ID	0030-MT	0045-SC	0043-PR
0017-IL	0031-NE	0046-SD	0059-Pac. Is. Ter.
0018-IN	0032-NV	0046-TN	0052-VI

If you are interested in all types of real property located **anywhere** in the 50 states and/or the District of Columbia, Puerto Rico, the U.S. Virgin Islands, American Samoa, Guam, or the U.S. Pacific trust territories, check the box under **All Locations and Types.** You will then receive all notices issued by all of GSA's regional real estate sales offices.

— —

Notices of Individual Sales

Mail to: U.S. General Services Administration (9KS)
525 Market Street
San Francisco, CA 94105

If you would like to receive notices of individual sales of Federal real estate property, complete the appropriate items and mail this form to the address above.

Type of Property (Check one or more boxes)

❑ Agriculture, timber, grazing   ❑ Industrial
and minerals
❑ Commercial   ❑ Residential

Location of Property (Write in the four-digit numbers from the list opposite of the locations for which you wish to receive sales notices.)

_ _ _ _ Location   _ _ _ _ Location   _ _ _ _ Location

❑ *All locations and types*

Name and Address for Notices (Please print clearly):

NAME_____

STREET_____ APT. OR SUITE_____

CITY_____ STATE_____ ZIP_____

12.0 <u>THE SMALL BUSINESS ADMINISTRATION</u>

The SBA is another governmental arm that loans money for properties and is sometimes forced into a position of foreclosure. SBA loans cover a myriad of business enterprises: everything from retail shops to restaurants. Each state is responsible for its own auctions and sales. On the following pages is a list of SBA offices nationwide; if you are interested in obtaining information regarding upcoming auctions or types of property to be auctioned, you can either write or call the Chief of Liquidation for your areas of interest.

SMALL BUSINESS ADMINISTRATION FIELD OFFICES

STATE	CITY	ZIP	ADDRESS	PUBLIC PHONE
Region 1:				
CT	Hartford	06106	330 Main Street, 2nd Floor	(203) 240-4700
MA	Boston	02110	155 Federal Street, 9th Floor	(617) 451-2023
MA	Boston	02222	10 Causeway Street, Room 265	(617) 565-5590
MA	Springfield	01103	1550 Main Street, Room 212	(413) 785-0268
ME	Augusta	04330	40 Western Avenue, Room 512	(207) 622-8378
NH	Concord	03302	55 Pleasant Street, Room 210	(603) 225-1400
RI	Providence	02903	380 Westminster Mall, 5th Floor	(401) 528-4561
VT	Montpelier	05602	87 State Street, Room 205	(802) 828-4474
Region 2:				
NJ	Camden	08104	2600 Mt. Ephrain Avenue	(609) 757-5183
NJ	Newark	07102	60 Park Place, 4th Floor	(201) 645-2434
NY	Albany	12207	445 Broadway, Room 222	(518) 472-6300
NY	Buffalo	14202	111 W. Huron Street, Room 1311	(716) 846-4301
NY	Elmira	14901	333 E. Water Street, 4th Floor	(607) 734-8130
NY	Melville	11747	35 Pinelawn Road, Room 102E	(516) 454-0769
NY	New York	10278	26 Federal Plaza, Room 31-08	(212) 264-7772
NY	New York	10278	26 Federal Plaza, Room 3100	(212) 264-4355
NY	Rochester	14614	100 State Street, Room 601	(716) 263-6700
NY	Syracuse	13260	100 S. Clinton Street, Room 1071	(315) 423-5383
PR	Hato Rey	00915	Carlos Chardon Avenue, Room 691	(809) 766-4002
VI	St. Croix	00820	4C & 4D Este Sion Frm, Room 7	(809) 778-5380
VI	St. Thomas	00801	Veterans Drive, Room 283	(809) 774-8530
Region 3:				
DC	Washington	20036	1111 18th Street, 6th Floor	(202) 634-1500
DE	Wilmington	19801	920 N. King Street, Suite 412	(302) 573-6295
MD	Baltimore	21202	10 N. Calvert Street, 3rd Floor	(301) 962-4392
PA	Harrisburg	17101	100 Chestnut Street, Room 309	(717) 782-3840
PA	King of Prussia	19406	475 Allendale Road, Suite 201	(215) 962-3700
PA	King of Prussia	19406	475 Allendale Road, Suite 201	(215) 962-3846
PA	Pittsburgh	15222	960 Penn Avenue, 5th Floor	(412) 644-2780
PA	Wilkes-Barre	18702	20 N. Pennsylvania Avenue, Room 2327	(717) 826-6497
VA	Richmond	23240	400 N. 8th Street, Room 3015	(804) 771-2617
WV	Charleston	25301	550 Eagan Street, Suite 309	(304) 347-5220
WV	Clarksburg	26301	168 W. Main Street, 5th Floor	(304) 623-5631

Continued on next page

STATE	CITY	ZIP	ADDRESS	PUBLIC PHONE
Region 4:				
GA	Atlanta	30367	1375 Peachtree St. NE, 5th Floor	(404) 347-2797
GA	Statesbro	30458	52 N. Main Street, Room 225	(912) 489-8719
FL	Tampa	33602	501 East Polk Street, Suite 104	(813) 228-2594
FL	W. Palm Beach	33407	5601 Corporate Way S., Suite 402	(407) 689-3922
GA	Atlanta	30309	1720 Peachtree Rd NW, 6th Floor	(404) 347-4749
AL	Birmingham	35203	2121 8th Avenue N, Suite 200	(205) 731-1344
NC	Charlotte	28202	222 S. Church Street, Room 300	(7040 371-6563
SC	Columbia	29202	1835 Assembly Street, Room 358	(803) 765-5376
FL	Coral Gables	33146	1320 S. Dixie Highway, Suite 501	(305) 536-5521
MS	Jackson	39201	100 W. Capitol Street, Suite 400	(601) 965-5325
FL	Jacksonville	32256	7825 Haymeadows Way, Suite 100-B	(904) 670-1910
KY	Louisville	40202	600 Dr. M.L.K. Jr. Pl., Room 188	(502) 582-5976
TN	Nashville	37228	50 Vantage Way, Suite 201	(615) 736-7176
MS	Gulfport	39501	One Hancock Plaza, Suite 1001	(601) 863-4449
Region 5:				
IL	Chicago	60604	219 S. Dearborn Street, Room 437	(312) 353-4528
IL	Chicago	60604	230 S. Dearborn Street, Room 510	(312) 353-0359
IL	Springfield	62704	511 W. Capitol Street, Suite 302	(217) 492-4416
IN	Indianapolis	46204	429 N. Pennsylvania St., Suite 100	(317) 226-7272
MI	Detroit	48226	477 Michigan Avenue, Room 515	(313) 226-6075
MI	Marquette	49885	300 S. Front Street	(906) 225-1108
MN	Minneapolis	55403	100 N. 6th Street, Suite 610	(612) 370-2324
OH	Cincinnati	45202	550 Main Street, Room 5028	(513) 684-2814
OH	Cleveland	44199	1240 E. 9th Street, Room 317	(216) 522-4180
OH	Columbus	43215	85 Marconi Boulevard	(614) 469-6860
WI	Eau Claire	54701	500 S. Barstow Commo, Room 17	(715) 834-9012
WI	Madison	53703	212 E. Washington Avenue, Room 213	(608) 264-5261
WI	Milwaukee	53203	310 W. Wisconsin Avenue, Suite 400	(414) 291-3941
Region 6:				
AR	Little Rock	72201	320 W. Capitol Ave., Room 601	(501) 378-5871
LA	New Orleans	70112	1661 Canal Street, Suite 2000	(504) 589-6685
LA	Shreveport	71101	500 Fannin Street, Room 8A-08	(318) 226-5196
NM	Albuquerque	87102	625 Silver Ave., SW, Suite 320	(505) 755-6185
OK	Oklahoma City	73102	200 N.W. 5th Street, Suite 670	(405) 231-4301
TX	Austin	78701	300 E. 8th Street, Room 520	(512) 482-5288
TX	Corpus Christi	78401	400 Mann Street, Suite 403	(512) 888-3331
TX	Dallas	75235	8625 King George Dr., Bldg. C	(214) 767-7643
TX	Dallas	75242	1100 Commerce St., Room 3C-36	(214) 767-0608
TX	El Paso	79935	10737 Gateway W., Suite 320	(915) 541-7586
TX	Ft. Worth	76102	819 Taylor Street, Room 8A-27	(817) 334-3777
TX	Harlingen	78550	222 East Van Buren St., Rm 500	(512) 427-8533
TX	Houston	77054	2525 Murworth, Suite 112	(713) 660-2421
TX	Lubbock	79401	1611 Tenth Street, Suite 200	(806) 743-7462
TX	Marshall	75670	505 E. Travis	(214) 935-5257
TX	San Antonio	78216	7400 Blanco Road, Suite 200	(512) 229-4535

STATE	CITY	ZIP	ADDRESS	PUBLIC PHONE
Region 7:				
IA	Cedar Rapids	52402	373 Collins Road NE, Room 100	(319) 393-8630
IA	Des Moines	50309	210 Walnut Street, Room 749	(515) 284-4762
KS	Wichita	67202	110 E. Waterman Street	(316) 269-6273
MO	Kansas City	64105	323 W. 8th Street, Suite 501	(816) 374-6762
MO	Kansas City	64106	911 Walnut Street, 13th Floor	(816) 426-3608
MO	Springfield	65802	620 S. Glenstone St., Suite 110	(417) 864-7670
MO	St. Louis	63101	815 Olive Street, Room 242	(314) 539-6600
NE	Omaha	68154	11145 Mill Valley Road	(402) 221-3604
Region 8:				
CO	Denver	80201	721 19th Street, Room 407	(303) 844-6501
CO	Denver	80202	999 18th Street, Suite 701	(303) 294-7001
MT	Helena	59626	301 S. Park	(406) 449-5381
ND	Fargo	58108	657 Second Ave. N., Room 218	(701) 239-5131
SD	Sioux Falls	57102	101 S. Main Ave., Suite 101	(605) 336-4231
UT	Salt Lake City	84138	125 S. State Street, Room 2237	(801) 524-5800
WY	Casper	82602	100 East B Street, Room 4001	(307) 261-5761
Region 9:				
AZ	Phoenix	85004	2005 N. Central Ave., 5th Floor	(602) 379-3732
AZ	Tucson	85701	300 W. Congress Street, Room 3V	(602) 670-6715
CA	Fresno	93727	2719 N. Air Fresno Dr.	(209) 487-5189
CA	Glendale	91203	330 N. Grand Blvd., Suite 1200	(213) 894-2956
CA	Sacramento	95814	660 J Street, Room 215	(916) 551-1426
CA	San Diego	92188	880 Front Street, Suite 4-S-29	(619) 557-5440
CA	San Francisco	94105	211 Main Street, 4th Floor	(415) 744-6804
CA	San Francisco	94105	71 Stevenson Street, 20th Floor	(415) 744-6409
CA	Santa Ana	92703	901 W. Civic Ctr. Dr., Suite 160	(714) 836-2494
CA	Ventura	93003	6477 Telephone Road, Suite 10	(805) 642-1866
GM	Agana	96910	Pacific Daily News Bldg, Room 508	(671) 472-7277
HI	Honolulu	96850	300 Ala Moana, Room 2213	(808) 541-2990
NV	Las Vegas	89125	301 E. Stewart St., Room 301	(702) 388-6611
NV	Reno	89505	50 S. Virginia Street, Room 238	(702) 784-5268
Region 10:				
AK	Anchorage	99513	222 W. 8th Avenue, Room A36	(907) 271-4022
ID	Boise	83702	1020 Main Street, Suite 290	(208) 334-1696
OR	Portland	97201	222 S.W. Columbia, Suite 500	(503) 326-2682
WA	Seattle	98121	2615 4th Avenue, Room 440	(206) 553-8544
WA	Seattle	98174	915 Second Avenue, Room 1792	(206) 553-5534
WA	Spokane	99204	W. 601 1st Avenue, 10th Floor E.	(509) 353-2807

13.0 FANNIE MAE AND AMERICAN HOME FINANCE

Fannie Mae (the Federal National Mortgage Association) is a stockholder owned, congressionally chartered corporation that was created to provide supplemental liquidity to the housing finance market. The nation's third largest corporation in terms of assets, Fannie Mae is also the largest source of conventional mortgage funds in the U.S.

Fannie Mae operates at the heart of the secondary mortgage market — a $300-400 *billion*-a-year industry. Fannie Mae purchases mortgage loans from local lenders, including mortgage banking companies, commercial banks, and savings and loan associations, with funds borrowed in the capital markets. In this way, Fannie Mae channels billions of dollars each year from the capital markets into home financing.

Fannie Mae also provides liquidity to the mortgage marketplace through its Mortgage-Backed Security (MBS) guarantee activities. The securities are backed by pools of home mortgages. The loans are originated by local lenders that then combine the mortgages into pools. Fannie Mae reviews the underwriting of the loans and issues the securities providing a 100% guarantee to the investor of timely payments on both principal and interest. When the Mortgage-Backed Securities are issued, the loans are converted into bond-like instruments that are traded in a very active market. It is not unusual to see a billion dollars of these securities traded in a week.

During the 1980's, the American housing finance system provided more than $2.5 trillion to home buyers to help finance home purchases. Before the end of the next decade, at least an additional $3 trillion is expected to be required for the same purpose.

Fannie Mae is one organization involved in raising these high volumes of capital needed.

The integrity of home mortgages in our country is essential to the continued attraction of new investment money. As a result, Fannie Mae is constantly pursuing ways in which to better serve its public. It has led the way by standardizing mortgage products and by encouraging the market to incorporate consumer protection features into all adjustable-rate mortgages (ARMs). While trying to improve the quality of credit in our home finance system, Fannie Mae is working to provide home buyers with the broadest possible range of prudently underwritten mortgages.

Occasionally Fannie Mae acquires homes through foreclosure. These properties were foreclosed when their owners were unable to meet their monthly mortgage obligations. These Fannie Mae homes are sometimes referred to as REO's (real estate owned), or repossessed houses.

Fannie Mae wants to sell these homes as quickly as possible in order to minimize the high cost of managing and holding properties. In order to do so, they frequently sell the homes at prices less than comparable to similar homes on the market. Their competitive selling prices can mean real savings to you!

The condition of Fannie Mae homes is similar to other homes for sale in the same area. Often time their selling program includes improvements to the home such as painting and new carpeting. They also have some fixer-uppers — homes that are in need of repair and are therefore priced accordingly.

Fannie Mae provides competitive financing for many of their homes. You can find financing elsewhere if you wish.

There is an 800 number you can call to request current Fannie Mae listings of REO's. You will need to have in mind a particular area, i.e. be able to tell them the county or city that interests you. At the present time the only properties they will give information for on the 800 number are located in Arizona, Florida, Louisiana, Oklahoma and Texas. If you are interested in properties in other areas, you can write for information to:

FANNIE MAE
P.O. BOX 1365
Baltimore, MD 21203

If you are interested in properties in the states currently being serviced by the 800 number, simply call: 1800-553-4636.

There is also an 800 number you can call if you would like additional information about Fannie Mae; just call 1-800-752-1080.

Make sure you contact a real estate agent.

When your listing(s) arrive from FNMA, you will typically find that each includes the following information:

- property address
- number of bedrooms/bathrooms
- list price*
- real estate agent
- phone number

So now call the agents of any properties that are of interest to you and visit them.

> *Note: Don't take this price too literally since many FNMA homes sell for *less than the stated price.*

Consider attending public auctions.

FNMA has found that many of its properties which are sold at auctions are being bought by first-time home buyers. So don't feel intimidated about attending an auction and don't be left out. Radio and newspaper advertising are often used to announce local public auctions, so check with any real estate agents who list FNMA properties.

Keep looking.

14.0 FINANCE COMPANY FORECLOSURES — BEFORE THEY'RE ADVERTISED

This little-used information can complement your knowledge of government loans to purchase homes. Open your telephone book to the yellow pages and look up REAL ESTATE LOANS. Call up every one of the finance companies and banks. Ask to speak with someone who handles foreclosures on defaulted real estate loans and ask if they have any "real estate owned" homes. This means the homes they have had to take back because they foreclosed on the loan. They will probably ask you what kind of property you're looking for, so be prepared with an answer: **"I'm looking for a single family two or three bedroom home"** or **"I'm trying to find some income property with one to five units"** or whatever you really are looking for.

Since finance companies are in the business of giving loans, not selling homes, they will be interested in getting the foreclosed homes off their books as soon as possible. Foreclosures look bad to their auditors. It means the bank made a bad decision when they made that particular home loan. And small, independent lenders simply can't afford to hold onto extra properties.

You should try to get on a mailing list if they have one, or get the name of the person in charge of foreclosures and give that person your name. Tell them you will keep in touch because you would like to buy a home at a good discount.

The homes will be offered at bargain prices for several reasons:

1)   the financial institution doesn't want to spend a lot of time and money advertising the home in order to get the best prices;

2)   all they have at stake is the price of the loan so they really don't care about getting more than that price;

3)   they will often give you a good deal on financing it — even a point or two below market interest rate and no money down just to turn it quickly from a liability to a money-making proposition for them again.

On the other hand, sometimes the financial institution doesn't want to see the property again or having anything to do with it, so they will require that you get your own financing. This is where your knowledge of government loans comes in. But you will have to act quickly, since they will not want to wait long.

Some savings and loans try to hold out for top market dollar and work only through real estate agents. If you are quoted a price on a property which you do not feel is particularly a bargain, go ahead and look at the property anyway. You can always make a lower offer which they may very well accept. Remember, they want to get the property off their hands, so *make the effort*. It may get you exactly what you want!

An important point: as we keep saying, CALL EVERY SINGLE FINANCE COMPANY. You will never cease to be amazed at the variety of answers you will get. NEVER assume that the answer of one will be the answer of all of them. Some finance companies are run by individual local businesspeople; others are part of a nationally-held firm. They all have their own peculiarities and differing goals. It really doesn't take that long to call them all, and it can mean a tremendous difference to you in dollars.

How To Find Hud-approved Lenders In Your Area

Certain lenders are approved by HUD to process HUD insured loans. These lenders will be familiar with a variety of programs and should be able to give you a good idea of whether you and the property you want to buy will qualify for a HUD-insured loan. The great thing about government loans is that they are completely assumable, and when you go to resell the property later, your buyer doesn't have to qualify. This will make it very easy to sell your home in the future. Another advantage of HUD-insured loans is that they generally require a smaller down payment than most bank loans.

HUD approves many lenders, but you will find that only a few of them are aware of the HUD programs. When you call, ask FIRST to speak to a loan officer. Ask the officer **"Do you, or does anyone in your company actively work with HUD-insured loans?"** If so, tell the officer what type of program you are interested in and they will tell you whether they work with that program or not. If they don't work with that specific program, they may be able to help you with an alternate program that may be more suitable for you.

Always be willing to listen to what other people are saying, even if at first you don't think it applies to you.

The government has given their approved lenders the right to completely process the loan application before submitting it to the HUD office for final approval. This way, the lending institutions can process loans more quickly, allowing the mortgages to close within a shorter time.

The lenders charge "points" to process the loan — this means each point charged is 1% of the total loan amount borrowed. On a $100,000 loan, for example, 1 point would cost $1,000. At the time of this writing, the points for a 10% loan were generally about 2 points. When you call the lenders, ask **every single one of them** what they are charging for the loans. Not only the interest rate, but the points charged, the loan origination fee, appraisal fee, etc. Each lender charge different amounts, depending on whether or not they want to encourage the type of loan you are interested in at the time you call them. **This can make a difference of a lot of money,** so it is very important to you that you take the time to call each and every lender.

Currently rates of 11-12% are typical of 30-year fixed rate mortgages currently being offered by various lenders. The adjustable rate mortgage (ARM) starts low and is increased up to and agreed-upon amount — a 5% "cap" is standard. Your rate can start at, say 8½%, and over a period of time would increase to 13½%. Your payments will end up higher but you will probably be earning more and be comfortable in handling a larger payment in a few years as the rate is adjusted. Today's adjustable rate mortgages are usually assumable, which means when you sell your house the new buyer can "assume" or take over your mortgage. A buyer will sometimes be required to be prequalified to assume your mortgage on a standard loan, in contrast to the HUD-insured loans in which prequalification is not normally necessary.

15.0 <u>MINOR REPAIRS TO THE HOME YOU OWN</u>

<u>FHA Title I Loan</u>

The government is concerned about you keeping up the house you now own. It does the government no good for neighborhoods to become run down and neglected because the homeowners cannot afford to do the repairs required.

To help these homeowners, FHA (Federal Housing Administration) has a Title I Loan which is very easy to get in some areas (all areas are different; check with local lenders). For $2,500 or less, you often don't need any security for the loan. Title I Loans are made in amounts up to $17,500 for up to 15 years, although a lien will be put against your home to ensure a larger loan is repaid as agreed.

This money may be used to make a variety of repairs on your house: anything that will make it more liveable and useful. You can even use them for such items as garbage disposals, dishwashers, washers and dryers, refrigerators, built-in ovens and any energy conserving or solar energy systems. The hope of the government is that you will make the small repairs needed as you go along, rather than let your home get very run down and finally need major work, which would be far more costly.

As we have said earlier in this book, everyone benefits from homes being owned and kept up nicely. Well-tended homes raise the neighborhood standards and create a ripple effect; that is, your neighbors will often follow suit when they see your home being spruced up. Also, when homeowners are busy repairing their homes, it increases the employment in the area, more money is spent on the materials required and the entire community becomes more prosperous and healthy.

To find a lender of an FHA Title I Loan, call lenders on your HUD-approved list and talk to a loan officer. Ask the loan officer whether they issue FHA Title I loans; if they do, tell the officer how much you want to borrow and ask what the interest rates are. Interest rates will be different from lender to lender, and the only way you'll know which has the <u>best</u> rates is to check them out. The only requirements are that you own your home (or have a long-term lease on it), have a satisfactory credit rating, and have enough income to repay the loan. You will receive your answer within a very few days on this type of loan. Since the interest rates can be low and the terms generous, you may find it extremely beneficial to get small amounts of money this way.

The reason the HUD-approved lenders can afford to lend the money at very low rates of interest is because they are assured by the U.S. Government that it will pay them back in case you default on the loan. This gives them security, so they can lower the interest rates for you since they are not taking a gamble on whether they will get the money back or not.

16.0 HUD GIVES MONEY TO COMMUNITIES SO THEY CAN PROVIDE AFFORDABLE HOUSING

Title I Grants

This program is called **The Joint Venture for Affordable Housing** and was established to encourage local building officials and home builders to work together with the citizens of their community to overcome costly local regulations. It is the opinion of HUD that many of the local building codes are excessive and unnecessary and if they were simplified and made less stringent, housing could be affordable for a larger segment of the population. Most communities have a certain lot size requirement, but HUD says the lots shouldn't have to be so large. They also feel that many of the regulations were made long ago before modern materials which are better and less expensive were available, so the codes should be changed to reflect this.

In the past couple of years there have been 29 demonstration projects throughout the country to show that the costs can be cut by as much as 20% using better planning and design and more economical construction techniques. HUD will send trained representatives to the communities to advise them of the successful cost-cutting techniques so the communities can take advantage of them and provide more affordable housing for their citizens.

Cities with populations of at least 50,000 and qualified urban counties with populations of at least 200,000 can apply for a Title I grant from HUD. The amount HUD will give them depends on their situation, which generally is decided based upon the community need, amount of housing over-crowding, age of housing available, the poverty level of the community and so forth.

The community agency (it can be a non-profit organization or a city or county government agency which is in charge of the program) needs to submit a copy of their ideas for utilizing the funds from HUD. They need to have a well-defined community development program in mind and would have to promise to follow a Housing Assistance Plan approved by HUD.

Once the agency receives the funds, they then must inform the citizens of their community about the funds available (usually called Community Development Block Grant programs) and what the general parameters HUD sets for using the funds. Appendix 5 (page 108) is just such an announcement

114

which was placed in the paper here in Santa Barbara. They next have a meeting and come up with a tentative program for using the funds and publish this proposed statement so the citizens may have an opportunity to comment on it and add their ideas. They make a final version of the plan which incorporates the citizen views they received.

On the next page is an advertisement (Figure 1) cut from an issue of the Los Angeles Times newspaper. You notice it says "YOU MAY QUALIFY FOR A HOUSING SUBSIDY BY THE COMMUNITY REDEVELOPMENT AGENCY OF LOS ANGELES." That is how the Community Development Department has chosen to utilize some of their HUD funds. Also notice that they are granting a subsidy to people so that their housing payment, including miscellaneous fees, comes to no more than 30% of their monthly income. Also notice that the interest rate is only 10.6% fixed for 30 years, while at the time the ad was published the standard interest rate was around 13%. In our example if you paid 13% interest, your payments and interest would be more than $750 per month (versus $613.75 per month at 10.6% interest).

YOU MAY QUALIFY FOR A HOUSING SUBSIDY BY THE COMMUNITY REDEVELOPMENT AGENCY OF LOS ANGELES.

NEW ONE BEDROOM ONE BATH

Household income:
  Not less than $1,500.00 per month.
  Not more than $2,879.00 per month.

10.6% **Fixed interest rate for 30 years.**
(11.46% Annual Percentage Rate)

EXAMPLE	Cost $70,000	P&I	$613.75
	Downpayment 5% 3,500	Assoc. Fee	$106.16
		Taxes	72.92
	Mortgage $66,500	PMI	$33.25
			$826.08
	Subsidy at $1,500 income level		333.00
	Monthly payment, only		**$493.08**

FOR ADDITIONAL INFORMATION & QUALIFICATION CALL
  (213)   BETWEEN 12 NOON AND 5 PM
ONLY THREE CONDOMINIUMS LEFT!!!

17.0 TAX-EXEMPT REVENUE BONDS MEAN FUNDS FOR YOU

Each state, county and city can pass tax-exempt revenue bonds to raise funds for housing. (See Appendix 6, page 109, for an example.) They then use the money to provide direct loans for the development of new rental and cooperative multi-family housing for low and moderate-income households. They also use the money to help moderate and low income families buy or improve properties in targeted areas by providing them loans at below market interest rates.

The direct loans are made to developers (90% mortgage loans) and non-profit agencies (100% financing) who want to construct or rehabilitate apartment or housing complexes for low-income families, elderly, etc. The projects are then subsidized by the HUD Section 8 Program (see Chapter 15) and 30% of the tenants must be very low income, which means their income does not exceed 50% of the median income for the area.

The other type of thing is for Home Ownership and Home Improvement Loans with the funds made available to fix up housing in certain areas. The homeowners get loans at below market rates (currently in California, the usual rates for this type of loan are 10-11%). The loans are made through private lenders but guaranteed by the government.

The purpose of making these funds available is to inject new life into deteriorating neighborhoods, help low income families become homeowners, and to make a supply of affordable housing available to a larger segment of the population.

This money can be used to buy, buy and rehabilitate, refinance an existing loan and rehabilitate, or just rehabilitate. The interest rate varies according to the bond sales the area has had, so sometimes the interest rate will be very low, other times, just a little below market.

If the loan will be guaranteed by FHA or VA, your down payment would only be 3-4%; if it is through the standard mortgage institution, 10% will be required, and the down payment can be 5% if your credit meets the approval of the lender and the private mortgage insurer.

Developers are welcome to use this fund for their projects. They must have the project in a Concentrated Rehabilitation Area (CRA) - a neighborhood inside a city which has been specially marked for upgrading. The agency will offer a more comprehensive financial package, but they will require that the rents be kept at a certain limit for 5 years. If a developer wants to rehabilitate a single family home in a CRA, it must be <u>vacant</u> for at least 90 days and be for sale at the time the developer applies for the money. There are no income limitations on developers, as long as they are going to make the housing available to low income families.

Since these funds are made available only periodically, the best way to find out about them is keeping an eye on your local newspaper for ads or articles which mention the funding (see Appendix 6, page 185).

18.0 THE URBAN DEVELOPMENT ACTION GRANT

Contact Your Local Housing Authority And Ask About This Program

The Urban Development Action Grant (UDAG) program attempts to help communities which are distressed or have pockets of distress to help stimulate the economy in these areas by encouraging public and private investment. The idea is that once some rehabilitation starts in the distressed area, other people will start to fix up other places in that area.

Even though a city may be generally prosperous, it might have an area it would like to see improved. The requirement is that at least 10% of the city's population live in this area and their income is less than 80% of the median income level for the area and 30% of those people have incomes below the poverty level.

This is a popular program, with 1,009 cities participating so far. These cities have received over $4 billion in Action Grant funding. That's an average of 20 cities per state. More than one-third of these funds are used in the Community Development Block Grant programs at the local level. Additionally, many states develop their own programs and have these funds in addition to the UDAG money.

The Federal Government gives the grants to the cities. The city then uses the Action Grant to stimulate the economy in the desired area of the city. They can use the money toward commercial, industrial or residential projects if they wish.

You can find out if the funds are available in your area by calling your LOCAL housing agency and asking them whether they have **Urban Development Action Grant Funds**. Ask if they are using any of the funds to assist people in buying homes. You might be able to help solve the city's problem and yours at the same time.

19.0 FARMER'S HOME ADMINISTRATION HAS MONEY, TOO!

The Farmer's Home Administration (**FmHA**, <u>not</u> to be confused with FHA) helps people in rural areas in all sorts of ways. They give grants, guarantee loans and supply technical advice and assistance to farmers and people living in rural areas of the United States.

19.1 Farms and Farmland

FmHA will send a farm expert out (they very likely have a field office in your area if you live in a rural area) to help you analyze your needs and advise you which program best suits your needs and what to do next. Each loan is tailored to the individual situation. Special emphasis is given to helping farmers who are just getting started and have limited credit and income at the time they are applying for the loan.

Family-sized farms are eligible for this assistance, and they can be owned by individuals, cooperatives or corporations. As is the case with the HUD insured loans, you need to apply to a regular lending institution, which processes your loan application, then contacts FmHA after the paper work is done.

You can use the money to buy a farm, add to one you already own, make some improvements such as buildings, develop the land, buy farm equipment, put in drainage, drill wells, clear trees.

You can even use the money to set up a riding stable, make a lake, set up a boating and camping area, have a souvenir shop, service station, or any other number of recreation-oriented businesses you could run in your area.

The interest rates are set according to the person's ability to pay. The maximum term of the loan would be 40 years. If you really can't afford to make payments at first, there is even a program for you. They will review your situation periodically and you will be expected to start repaying as soon as you are able.

These loan funds are really meant just to help you get started, and when you are financially on your feet, they expect you to refinance through a regular lender and pay off the FmHA loan.

So, if you qualify:

- You have farm experience or training and the FmHA representative feels you possess the determination and have the ability to make a success of your plan,

- You are a citizen of the U.S., Puerto Rico, the U.S. Virgin Islands, American Samoa or the Commonwealth of the Northern Mariana Islands,

- You are legally able to be liable for the loan,

- You have tried unsuccessfully to get a loan through normal channels,

- Your farm will be no larger than an owner-operator size after you get the loan,

- You really need the income which would be provided by the farm or recreational business you would be setting up,

and you should apply at your nearest Farmer's Home Administration office. Look in your local telephone book under UNITED STATES GOVERNMENT, DEPARTMENT OF AGRICULTURE. If you cannot find one in your immediate area, then you can contact the head office in Washington, D.C. and they will tell you where the closest office is. Their address and phone number is:

FARMER'S HOME ADMINISTRATION
U.S. DEPARTMENT OF AGRICULTURE
WASHINGTON, D.C. 20250
202/447-4323

A representative will talk with you to determine what your needs are and which program you will need to apply for. He or she probably will come out to visit your farm, or the farm you intend to buy; you will be advised on the best procedure for setting it up or making the changes you are interested in. If you have outstanding debts, he can sometimes contact your creditors and arrange to have the payment delayed until you get on your feet or at least consolidate your payments and have them extended over a longer period of time to give you a break.

The loan will be secured by the farmland and the maximum amount is usually $200,00 to $300,000. The loan cannot be for more than the value of the farm or equipment you are buying.

If you have a job, you can still qualify for help if you can prove that you need the extra income to provide a decent standard of living for yourself and your family.

19.2 Single Family Dwellings

FmHA also has programs in some areas to assist in the purchase of rural (non-farm) homes when you and the property meet certain conditions. For you to qualify, you must meet the following standards:

- You must be a citizen of the U.S. and 18 years of age

- You must not, at present, own a home

- You must personally occupy your FmHA home on a permanent basis

- You must be unable to obtain a loan from a conventional lender

- Total household income must not exceed $23,500 per year (gross income minus 5% and minus $300 for every child under 18 years living in the home) -- these figures may differ from area to area

- You should be permanently employed and have exceeded standard employee probationary period

- You must have an established rent history showing prompt rent payment

- Loan amount must be within your repayment ability, typically between $50,000 and $60,000 (figures may differ for your area)

For the property to qualify, it must satisfy the following conditions:

- Existing dwelling or proposed building site must be in a rural area with a population of 10,000 or less

- A house lot must be located on a publicly maintained road and be one acre or less

- New or existing houses must be modest in size, design and cost; amenities such as dishwashers and garbage disposals are prohibited; 2-car garages in new construction are prohibited

- The dwelling must contain no more than 1,200 square feet of living area (this may be adjusted for larger families)

- Selling price of the house to be purchased or lot and dwelling to be built should not exceed $60,000 (this figure may differ from area to area)

- House and contractors must be approved by FmHA

There is no charge for applying for these FmHA loans. If your loan application is accepted, however, there will be a loan initiation fee for the appraisal and other paperwork that must be done to get the loan processed.

19.3 Rural Rental Housing

FmHA has a program available to benefit both investors and renters. This program provides loans to individuals, partnerships, profit and/or non-profit corporations to build, purchase or repair multiple unit rental housing. The property would then be rented to eligible low and moderate income families and also to individuals over the age of 62.

The following list explains the qualifications needed to obtain a loan from the FmHA for this program:

- The rural community cannot have a population larger than 20,000.

- You must agree to rent units to eligible individuals and families.

- You must not be able to finance the project with personal resources.

- You must be able to furnish FmHA with cost estimates and detailed plans for the project.

There are some special restrictions/terms regarding the loan:

- There is a maximum period of 50 years for repayment of the loan.

- Loans will not be for more than 95 percent of the appraisal value or development cost, whichever is less.

- The amount of rent charged will have to be affordable for eligible occupants.

- Rental income will have to be deposited in special accounts and reserve funds will have to be maintained for long-term capital replacement needs.

Contact the FmHA county office to find out if this program is available in the area you are interested in. For further information, you can also contact Farmers Home Administration, U.S. Department of Agriculture, Washington, D.C. 20250.

20.0 <u>WHEN YOU ASK FOR INFORMATION, WHAT YOU CAN EXPECT TO RECEIVE</u>

While we wish that we could tailor this book to meet each and every reader's personal needs, obviously, we'd have quite a task (not to mention a book too large to send via mail!) What we have done is request information from one city — one that's pretty much smack-dab in the middle of the country — so that you can see the types of information which is available regarding low to moderate income housing.

This information, which appears on the following pages, also contains the current Median Income Guidelines for the HUD programs, which should be of interest to you as well.

HOUSING AND COMMUNITY SERVICES IN DES MOINES

HOUSING & COMMUNITY SERVICES DEPARTMENT

The Community Services Division utilizes Federal, State and local public and private funds for outreach, information, referral, advocacy and direct services for low and moderate income persons who live in Des Moines. This division also operates several energy assistance projects and the weatherization program. Support services are also provided to neighborhood boards and organizations.

The Housing Services Division works to preserve the City's housing stock through housing rehabilitation activities and safety inspections of rental properties. Services are also available for persons needing handicapped housing, financial counseling for dealing with delinquent mortgages, or homeless persons in need of shelter.

To find us in the telephone book, look in the blue pages under the City of Des Moines:

Housing & Community Services or Neighborhood Site Offices

COMMUNITY SERVICES PROGRAMS

CITIZEN PARTICIPATION

Provides support services to the Central Advisory Board, the Neighborhood Priority Boards and other neighborhood groups and organizations.

ENERGY ASSISTANCE

Helps pay a portion of winter heating bills.

WEATHERIZATION

Insulation and other conservation materials are installed in homes to save energy.

FAMILY DEVELOPMENT

Provides families an opportunity to set goals for change.

TELEPHONE SERVICE COUNSELING AND SILVER THREAD

Provides information on the most economical telephone services and discounts available to households.

GARDEN PROJECT

Provides seeds, plants and rototilling.

FAN PROGRAM

Fans are loaned to provide heat relief.

UTILITY ASSISTANCE

Payment planning services, arrange deposits, reconnection.

FOOD PANTRY

Provides emergency food or makes referral to closest pantry.

SURPLUS FOOD

Surplus foods are distributed four times yearly.

JOB SERVICE

Weekly or daily hours for job service representatives at site offices.

HOUSING SERVICES PROGRAMS

HOUSING SAFETY ACTIVITIES

- Enforces federal, state and municipal housing ordinances.

- Inspects rental units city-wide.

- Responds to citizen complaints of housing conditions.

- Secures vacant/abandoned structures.

- Issues certificates for Des Moines Public-Housing Authority rental units.

HOUSING REHABILITATION ACTIVITIES

- **Administers Neighborhood Conservation Strategy.**

  - Home Improvement Loan Program
  - 312 Loan Program
  - Deferred Maintenance Program
  - Apartment Improvement Program
  - Dunham Street Program
  - Architectural Barrier Removal
  - Handicapped Housing Program
  - Services for Homeowners Program (SHOP)
  - Technical Assistance on housing rehabilitation for low-moderate income home owners.
  - Technical Assistance for home purchase and repair loans from private lending institutions & non-profits.

Housing and Community Services Neighborhood Site Offices

Central Office
East First and Des Moines Street
283-4180

Logan/Four Mile
East 17th Court & Garfield
265-7225

Model Cities
1615 — 11th
283-4104

Southeast/Pioneer Columbus
2100 Southeast Fifth
283-4120

Woodland-Willkie
900 — 17th
283-4038

If you would like to volunteer to help us with any of our programs, please call one of the offices listed above.

The Department of Housing & Community Services receives funding from the City of Des Moines, HUD Community Development Block Grant, the State of Community Services & Energy Block Grants, United Way, private donations, I CARE and contractual arrangements with local utilities.

	Home Improvement Loan Program	Deferred Maintenance Loan Program	Architectural Barrier Removal Program	Section 312 Loan Program	Rental Rehabilitation Program (rental units)
Property must be In Target Area	yes	no	no	yes*	yes*
Completed project must meet HQS	yes	no	no	yes	yes
Direct Loan	15 years			n/a	n/a
Deferred Payment Lien	15 years	5 years	5 years	mortgage	10 years
Eligible Applicants:					
Owner-Occupied	yes	yes	yes	yes	no
Investor-Owner	no	no	no	yes	yes
Maximum Loan Amount	$15,000	$3,500	$4,500	$33,500/unit	per size of unit
Applicant must be low-mod. Income	yes (80%*)	yes (50%)	yes (80%)	no	no
Waiting List for Applicants?	yes	yes	no	yes	no

* See Housing Rehabilitation Handbook or Contact Housing & Community Services Department for more specific Information (283-4180)

** Small targeted area in SE/Pioneer Columbus Neighborhood

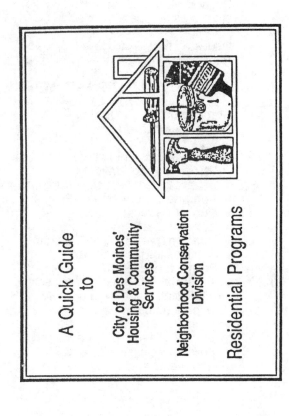

A Quick Guide
to

City of Des Moines'
Housing & Community Services

Neighborhood Conservation Division

Residential Programs

For more information and program applications, please contact :

- Housing & Community Services Dept.
Armory Bldg., East First and Des Moines Sts.
Des Moines, Ia. 50307   (515) 283-4180

- Housing & Community Services Target Area Site Offices:
  - Woodland-Willkie -- 283-4038
  - Model Cities -- 283-4104
  - Pioneer Columbus/Southeast -- 283-4120
  - Logan/Four Mile --. 265-7225

Most programs are funded with Community Development Block Grant funds. The programs are developed through the Central Advisory Board and Neighborhood Priority Boards.

NEED FINANCIAL ASSISTANCE IN REPAIRING AN APARTMENT HOUSE OR OTHER RESIDENTIAL RENTAL PROPERTY?

THE APARTMENT IMPROVEMENT PROGRAM CAN PROVIDE A

NO INTEREST, DEFERRED PAYMENT LOAN

FOR UP TO 50% OF THE COST OF REPAIRS

No Assistance For 1 Bedroom or Efficiencies
(Up to $7,500 per 2-bedroom unit)
(Up to $8,500 per 3 or more bedroom unit)

LOAN FUNDS CAN BE USED FOR:

- Correcting Housing Code Violations

- Other essential repairs, including energy related repairs and improvements to aid the handicapped

- Architectural, engineering, legal, permit & related professional fees associated with the rehabilitation project

- Relocation payments to displaced tenants

- Financing costs such as loan origination fees, credit reports, title search and appraisal fees

LOANS AVAILABLE FOR PROPERTIES IN THE FOLLOWING TARGET AREAS:

WOODLAND-WILLKIE, MODEL CITIES, LOGAN,
PIONEER-COLUMBUS/SOUTHEAST

**FOR MORE INFORMATION CALL
HOUSING & COMMUNITY SERVICES DEPT.
CITY OF DES MOINES
283-4180**

130

Median Income Guidelines – H.I.L.P. Program

Family Size	25%	30%	35%	40%	45%	50%	55%
1	$6,625	$7,950	$9,275	$10,600	$11,925	$13,250	$14,575
2	$7,575	$9,090	$10,605	$12,120	$13,635	$15,150	$16,665
3	$8,525	$10,230	$11,935	$13,640	$15,345	$17,050	$18,755
4	$9,475	$11,370	$13,265	$15,160	$17,055	$18,950	$20,845
5	$10,063	$12,075	$14,088	$16,100	$18,113	$20,450	$22,138
6	$10,663	$12,795	$14,928	$17,060	$19,193	$22,000	$23,458
7	$11,250	$13,500	$15,750	$18,000	$20,250	$23,500	$24,750
8	$11,850	$14,220	$16,590	$18,960	$21,330	$25,000	$26,070

Family Size	60%	65%	70%	75%	80%	100%	120%
1	$15,900	$17,225	$18,550	$19,875	$21,200	$26,500	$31,800
2	$18,180	$19,695	$21,210	$22,725	$24,250	$30,300	$36,360
3	$20,460	$22,165	$23,870	$25,575	$27,250	$34,100	$40,920
4	$22,740	$24,635	$26,530	$28,425	$30,300	$37,900	$45,480
5	$24,150	$26,163	$28,175	$30,188	$32,200	$40,250	$48,300
6	$25,590	$27,723	$29,855	$31,988	$34,120	$42,650	$51,180
7	$27,000	$29,250	$31,500	$33,750	$36,000	$45,000	$54,000
8	$28,440	$30,810	$33,180	$35,550	$37,900	$47,400	$56,880

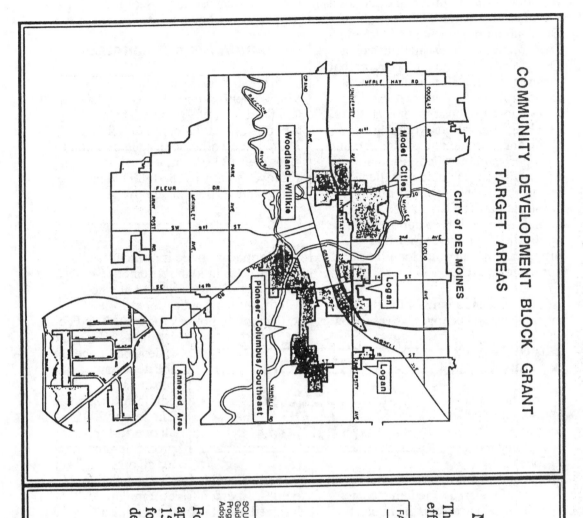

131

COMMUNITY DEVELOPMENT BLOCK GRANT TARGET AREAS

CITY of DES MOINES

Model Cities

Woodland–Willkie

Logan

Logan

Pioneer–Columbus/Southeast

Annexed Area

Median Income Guidelines

These median income guidelines are effective as of January 1988.

FAMILY SIZE	50%	80%	95%	100%
1	$13,250	$21,200	$25,200	$26,500
2	15,150	24,250	28,800	30,300
3	17,050	27,250	32,400	34,100
4	18,950	30,300	36,000	37,900
5	20,450	32,200	38,250	40,250
6	22,000	34,100	40,500	42,650
7	23,500	36,000	42,800	45,000
8	25,000	37,900	45,000	47,400

SOURCE: U.S. Department of Housing Urban Development Guidelines based on Section 8 Housing Assistance Payment Program for low (80%) and very low (50%) income families. Adopted February 16, 1990.

For the Section 312 Program, applicants may have an income up to 150% of the median. The interest rate for these Section 312 loans will vary, dependent on the applicant's income.

132

The Section 312 program operates as a cooperative venture between the U.S. Department of Housing and Urban Development (HUD) and the city of Des Moines. The Federal government furnishes the loan funds and services the loans. The City will process the loans and is responsible for such tasks as taking applications, verifying the applicant's income and credit, obtaining a property appraisal, cost estimate and work write-up, conducting settlement, and inspecting the property during construction. The City is also authorized by HUD to approve loan applications for one to four-unit properties, but all other loans must be approved by HUD.

The key components of the program, including recent changes, are as follows:

Interest Rates & Loan Terms

Three percent loans are available for owner-occupants of one-to-four-unit properties who have incomes below 80 percent of the area's median income. For all other borrowers, the interest rate is based on the yield of U.S. Treasury securities. One change in the interest rate policy relates to co-ops: a co-op now can get a 3 percent loan if all the units of the co-op are occupied by members of the co-op (except for units leased for less than three years by members who are away temporarily). In addition, 80 percent of the residents must have incomes below 80 percent of the median income of the area when they first occupy their units. For all other co-ops, the Section 312 loan must be made at the Treasury rate.

The maximum loan term is still either 20 years, or three-quarters of

the remaining usefully life of the property, whichever is less.

Maximum Loan Amounts

The limit has officially been raised to $33,500 per residential dwelling unit, up to a maximum of 99 units. The maximum for non-residential loans is $100,000. There are no other loan ceilings, but all loans over $200,000 now must be approved jointly by the HUD Field Office and HUD Headquarters.

Fees

An application fee is now charged to all borrowers at loan settlement (so applicants who are rejected or who withdraw their application prior to settlement do not pay the fee). The Fee is paid to HUD, and is designed to help the department offset its administrative costs. The fee is $200 for all one-to-four-unit properties and $300 for all other properties, and it may be included in the loan. A 1 percent risk premium, designed to help cover losses resulting from defaults, must be paid by all borrowers as part of their monthly payments.

Target Areas

Section 312 properties still must be in an area in which CDBG or UDAG funds are being spent, or in an Urban Homestead Area.

Eligible Borrowers and Properties

Individuals, corporations, and partnerships are all eligible borrowers.

SECTION 312 LOAN PROGRAM

Urban Homesteaders also are eligible borrowers, as are properly authorized co-ops. Eligible properties include singly family (both owner-occupied and investor-owned), multifamily, nonresidential and mixed use properties. Congregate housing and single-room occupancy properties also are eligible.

Eligible Loan Costs

Required Costs

As in the past, a Section 312 loan may not be made on a property unless the property has at least one code violation, and unless all such violations are repaired. One change is that the locality now can decide what the rehabilitation code will be. (If the locality has no local code, the Section 8 Housing Quality Standards will apply.) For 3 percent borrowers, the Section 312 loan must also include real estate taxes and hazard and flood insurance that come due or accrue during construction. (This is a required cost primarily because it helps protect HUD's security interest in the property.)

Other Eligible Costs

General property improvements are still eligible and are once again subject to the 40 percent rule; the total cost of all improvements which are not code items, or likely to become code items in the near future, cannot exceed 40 percent of the total Section 312 loan. Professional services required to obtain the loan, such as architectural and engineering services, are eligible as before. However, there are no longer maximum permissible amounts for these items, and they must simply be reasonable and

customary for the area. Refinancing also is eligible as long as the loan amount does not exceed the Section 312 maximum and the applicant's monthly payments without refinancing would not be excessive.

Ineligible Expenses

Local government administrative expenses, new construction, luxury items (i.e., items that substantially exceed those generally used in the area), and delinquent taxes related to the period prior to loan closing are all ineligible uses of 312 funds.

Review Process

Appraisals

An appraisal of the after-rehab value of the property is now required for all loans, with the following exception: appraisals are not required for loans fore one-to-four-unit properties of $33,500 or less if the most recently assessed value of the property is sufficient to meet the loan-to-value ration requirements described in the underwriting section below. Appraisals now can be done by qualified LPA staff for loans of $33,500 or less; outside fee appraisers are only required for loans over $33,500.

Work Write-Ups and Cost Estimates

A work write-up, which details all deficiencies and proposed work on the property, must be prepared for each Section 312 loan. Under the new rules, however, it may be prepared by a contractor, a qualified local government official or an independent fee inspector. If the contractor is the only one preparing a work write-up, the locality also must inspect the property and prepare a report listing all the deficiencies. A cost estimate must be prepared for each loan, and it should be prepared by a qualified local government official or an independent consultant in order to ensure that the proposed cost are reasonable.

Bidding

The Section 312 Program now only requires formal, competitive bidding for loans exceeding $100,000. All other loans may be formally or informally bid or negotiated, consistent with local policies. Borrowers, however, are strongly encouraged, regardless of the size of the loan, to obtain proposals from more than one contractor, which, again, helps ensure that the proposed costs are reasonable.

Underwriting

Some of the most important changes in the new handbook concern loan underwriting. For the first time, There will be quantifiable, national underwriting criteria. They are modeled on the standards used by Freddie Mac, and they are designed to ensure that loans are only made to borrowers likely to repay and where there is sufficient value in the property, in case the borrower defaults.

The criteria will be strictly enforced, although exceptions in extraordinary cases can be granted by HUD Field Offices. The new criteria will help ensure that funds are repaid so they can be re-lent to new borrowers, and that loans are not made to borrowers who cannot afford them, and who would be in danger of losing their homes in foreclosure proceedings if they

defaulted. In addition, under the new criteria, loans funds still can bemade to applicants in riskier neighborhoods at more attractive rates and for longer terms than conventional rehabilitation loans.

The criteria for both owner-occupants of one-to-four-unit properties and for investor-owned properties are summarized below.

Owner-Occupants of One-to-Four-Unit Properties

Affordability-Housing Expense and Debt Ratios

The borrower's gross income, rather than net income as in the past, is utilized, and housing costs do not include utilities or maintenance costs. The applicant's total monthly housing expenses (PITI) for the unit they occupy, including the repayment on the Section 312 loan and other debt secured by the property, cannot exceed 28 percent of gross monthly income. In addition, the applicant's long-term monthly debt, including all housing expensed detailed above, plus all the borrower's installment and the long-term debt, cannot exceed 36 percent of the gross monthly income.

Loan-to-Value Ratio Requirements

For borrowers getting 3 percent Section 312 loans, the discounted value of the Section 312 loan, plus the remaining balance of all other debt secured by the property which is senior to the 312 loan, cannot exceed 80 percent of the after-rehab appraised value of the property.

(For 20-year Section 312 loans made at 3 percent, 50 percent of the Section 312 loan amount is used for this calculation. For example, if a 3 percent-eligible borrower requests a 20 year Section 312 loan of $25,000 and if the total outstanding balance on other senior debt secured by the property is #20,000, the total debt for the Section 312 loan-to-value ratio would be $12,500 plus $20,000 or $32,500.)

For all other borrowers, the full amount of the Section 312 loan, plus the balance of all other debt secured by the property which is senior to the Section 312 loan, cannot exceed 90 percent of the after-rehab appraised value of the property.

Investor Loans

Affordability-Debt Coverage Ratio

Income from the property, rather than the borrower's personal income, is analyzed. Specifically, net operating income from the property) gross rental income, minus projected vacancies, minus all operating expenses except debt service) must be at least 110 percent of the total debt service on the property, including projected debt service on the Section 312 loan.

Loan-to-Value Ratio Requirements

For investor properties, the full amount of the Section 312 loan, plus the balance of all other debt secured by the property which is senior to the Section 312 loan, cannot exceed 90 percent of the after-rehab appraised value of the property.

Financial Interest in Property and Availability of Cash

The borrower must have at least 10 percent equity before and after rehab, and must have liquid assets equal to at least three months of debt service to cover contingencies and the lack of rental income during lease-up. Section 312 loans are now fully assumable if the assumptor meets all Section 312 eligibility requirements (including income limits for 3 percent loans) and all underwriting criteria.

HUD headquarters can waive income limits for a borrower seeking to assume a 3 percent loan if the existing loan is in danger of going into default. If not, a borrower seeking to assume a 3 percent loan whose income is higher than 80 percent of median can only do so if the borrower otherwise qualifies.

All applications for assumptions must be approved by HUD Headquarters.

Adapted from "Section 312 Rehabilitation Loans: Alive and Well," by Stuart Hershey, Journal of Housing. Volume 44, No. 2, March/April, 1987, pp. 75-79.

FOR FURTHER INFORMATION, CALL THE URBAN DEVELOPMENT DEPARTMENT, CITY OF DES MOINES AT 283-4180

21.0 DON'T BE AFRAID TO BE INNOVATIVE WHEN YOU'RE A FIRST-TIME HOME BUYER!

Part of the challenge of being a first-time home buyer is putting together a package that works for you, the amount of money you have saved, your credit stance, and the market in the area you wish to live. The following are a couple of approaches that have been used successfully by first-time homebuyers, and they just might be the plan for you, too.

WHAT IF YOU DON'T HAVE THE DOWN PAYMENT MONEY?

See if you can find someone who is willing to let you rent a house with an option to buy. If you can find a seller who is willing to work with you, you may be able to get into a new home by entering into a lease-option contract. Under this type of agreement, the buyer and seller usually sign a 6, 12 or 18 month lease for the property. They also sign a purchase contract spelling out the price, terms, and closing date, when hopefully there will be enough money to complete the deal.

This type of arrangement can work well for both buyer and seller, because the seller is receiving income from the property; the tenant has time to accumulate funds in order to close the sale, so they complement each other.

Usually in a lease-option agreement, you pay a set amount of money each month for rent, and an additional sum toward the downpayment. (i.e. let's say your lease payment is $500.00 per month, the contract may call for an additional $100.00 to go towards the downpayment). In some instances you will be required to put some money up front which is called "option funds". Option funds are negotiable, usually totaling 3 to 5% of the selling price. These option funds are held by the seller until the date which was set for the close of the sale, at which time this money and the extra $100 per month you've been paying are added together to become your downpayment. On the down side — if you don't exercise your option to purchase — they keep the option funds and the extra $100 a month you've been paying.

Many buyers are expected to prequalify for bank financing when going for a lease option, although this is not always the case.

A lease option arrangement gives the buyer an opportunity to get to know the house they are considering, the neighborhood, the school system, etc. It's sort of like trying it on for size. It also provides you with an opportunity to get other debts paid down during the option period.

Prior to signing any lease-option agreement, make sure you have your attorney take a look at it!

21.1 <u>Working As A Team To Accomplish Your Homeowning Dream</u>!

What if you're single and trying to buy a home? In today's market, it's hard enough for a two-income family to make that first purchase. But there's hope — if you're innovative and willing to work on the buddy-system.

Equity-sharing arrangements can be your key to owning your own home. If you are having trouble coming up with enough downpayment money, you may want to team up with another individual in similar circumstances. It may be a close friend, a family member — or someone you work with strictly as a business venture.

A simplified example of equity-sharing would be that two people pool their resources so that they can make the downpayment. Additionally, they agree to pay all of the bills 50/50.

Sometimes mom and dad are the partners in an equity-sharing situation, whereby they "loan" or "give" the downpayment to their son or daughter. In a situation like this the son or daughter pays the monthly mortgage, taxes and insurance and lives in the house. Both share in the home's equity and ownership. When the house is sold, the proceeds are split based on the percentage of ownership and whatever terms they agreed to up front.

Again, regardless of whether it's family, friend, etc., make sure that you have a contract that clearly spells out who gets what!

You can obtain additional tips for first-time homebuyers by sending a SELF-ADDRESSED STAMPED ENVELOPE TO:

Steve Crowley's Money Reports
P.O. Box 550
Fort Lauderdale, FL 33302

There is also a book available that talks in more detail about equity-sharing, entitled *THE EQUITY SHARING BOOK*, by Elaine St. James.

22.0 REAL ESTATE AS AN INVESTMENT

We talked earlier in this directory about how you should always look at real estate as an investment. Now we're going to let you read about how two people (Sylvia and Doug) have made real estate work for them. You'll want to read this section very carefully, because it truly contains the keys to financial independence for those of you who are willing to pay close attention!

Q: WHAT'S THE FIRST THING SOMEONE NEEDS TO DO IF THEY WANT TO INVEST IN REAL ESTATE?

A: They need to get a smart realtor, someone who's really on the ball. Someone who lives, eats and breaths real estate. We've been fortunate in finding someone who is single, and who truly loves her work. She is not the first realtor we used, but we use her exclusively now.

Q: ARE THERE ANY "RED FLAGS" THAT MIGHT GO UP WHEN YOU ARE DEALING WITH A REALTOR THAT MIGHT INDICATE THAT THEY AREN'T WORKING FOR YOU?

A: Follow through, detail. Whether they jump on something you mention and check it out, as opposed to hemming and hawing around. They should be listening to you as much as you listen to them. The other thing is that you need to give the realtor some fairly firm parameters on what you want, whether it's the county you want it in, the school district, the price range — and then see if the realtor follows these ground rules. If they start dragging you all over the countryside because they have a listing they want to unload, that's not the realtor for you. You need someone that uses the Multiple Listing Service (MLS) book. What you have to bear in mind, though, is that to a realtor, the seller is the client, and the realtor represents the client. They should have a fiduciary relationship with the buyer. If you are getting into real estate as a business, make sure you let the realtor know that you are not going to buy just one property. The advantage of working off of the MLS book is that it makes you the customer. Let them know that if they do right by you on the first property, you'll do right by them in the future by using them when you buy or sell.

Q: HOW DID YOU GET STARTED IN BUYING REAL ESTATE? I KNOW YOU'VE BOTH BEEN INVOLVED IN OTHER AREAS

OF ENDEAVOR — WAS THIS A PLAN YOU HAD ALL ALONG?

A: No, what happened was that we came back to this town to work. I had told lots of people over the years that they were crazy to stay in California and pay those ridiculous property taxes. I told them they were paying $7 - $8 - $9 thousand a year in taxes, and they could double that — take $7 thousand, $14 thousand and come back to the midwest and buy a beautiful home in a small town. I preached that for a number of years. When I came back here, this economy was really, really unique. You had a one-industry town that took it on the chin. They laid off half of their people at their major industry, the farm economy went into a tremendous demise, then they had union problems at the meat packing industry in town — they deunionized so people were making half of their previous wages. So here you had a really depressed economy. You had a lot of people burning down their houses to collect the insurance because they had a house that they paid $70,000 for and it was worth $25,000 on the market and they were out of work. People were losing their whole lives. These aren't like people out in California or New York — these are people whose great grandmothers and grandfathers were born here, their grandparents were born here — their parents were born here — and they believed in the system, and it killed them. They simply couldn't pull up roots and leave. What happened, which benefitted us and the community, and what turned this community around, was the Health Department. They began a policy whereby you either fixed up your property or you tore it down — or the Health Department would tear it down. This prevented the city from getting a lot of slum areas. Because of all the problems this city was having, the property values were roughly 30% of what they had been a few years previously.

Another dynamic that set the stage for this being a good area to invest in, was the fact that the old meat packing plant, although not union, employed 3 times as many people as it had previously (at half the wage), the other large manufacturer in town started hiring again, and the Japanese brought in a corn processing plant on the outskirts of town. This created a market where there were not enough rental houses, so they can rent for a high dollar amount, but the property values have not yet caught up. In other words, you can buy property really cheaply, turn it into a rental, and charge a good dollar amount for the property. You have people who can afford to pay the higher rents, but they can't save any money because they are paying the higher rents. Even if dad gave them the money to buy the house, their low income would not qualify them for the loan. Even though they're paying rents that are higher than what their house payment would be. It's a crazy thing — they're in a "Catch 22" situation.

Q: ARE THERE FEDERAL PROGRAMS IN THIS AREA THAT YOU KNOW OF?

A: There is very little of it here. Once in awhile you see a VA repo, but they go really quickly because of the terms. There is one tax program which is going currently that we're going to be involved in, and that is for deferment or cancellation of increased property taxes when you fix up a piece of property. You have to invest more than 10% of the assessed valuation of the property to fix it up, and there is a very limited area of town where it is applicable. I think they should have had a wider area, but they didn't ask me.

Q: HOW ABOUT THE FIRST HOUSE THAT YOU BOUGHT?

A: What happened was we bought our first house to live in. We hadn't planned on rentals. We had discussed rentals and thought that it might be a good idea to buy one or two just as a supplement to my pension if I retired at age 62. Well, I'm going to retire at 55, maybe 54, because our income has become so substantial off of rentals.

Q: BUT YOU HAD NO IDEA THIS WOULD BE THE CASE WHEN YOU STARTED?

A: No idea.

Q: HOW LONG AGO DID YOU BUY THE FIRST PROPERTY?

A: Two years ago — 1988 in September. We bought an old Victorian house for $32,000 and proceeded to fix it up cosmetically. Sylvia had a fair amount of experience with painting and wallpapering and decorating.

Q: DO YOU THINK THESE ABILITIES ARE IMPORTANT FOR PEOPLE WHO ARE GOING TO BUY RENTAL PROPERTY?

A: YES!!!! Cosmetics just sell a place. If they walk in and it looks good, most people assume that a place is structurally sound. So here we had bought this house for $32,000 — 18 inch brick walls, 2500 square feet, solid brick walls from the basement to the second floor — steam heat — a marble fireplace — 7 foot high mirror over the fireplace. We just couldn't believe it was that cheap. We thought that we had better take a close look at rentals — you know, buy a couple cheap and fix them up.

Q: DID YOU BUY THROUGH CONVENTIONAL MEANS?

A: We saw an ad in the paper, contacted the realtor, and bought the first rental house. We had a bad experience with the realtor. He didn't follow through on his contract on it and failed to get the termite inspection.

Q: WHAT KIND OF MONEY DID YOU INVEST?

A: Well, we had a little money at the time. We paid $30,000, financed 60%, ended up paying $12,000 down.

Q: WHICH IS A LOT MORE THAN MOST PEOPLE HAVE!

A: Yeah, right, and if we had it to do again we wouldn't have put that much down. All we had to do was paint one room and put some carpet into it. We began to figure our return on investment dollar. That's the key to rental properties, the return on investment dollar.

Q; DID YOU HAVE SOME FORMULA YOU USED?

A: Yeah, just a minute and I'll show you. We won't buy a place unless we can make at least 30% net a year on our investment dollar. Let me tell you what we've done for our son. He sold his house in Riverside, CA and made $35,000 profit. He wanted to go back and pick up his doctorate, but he has two small children and was having a hard time figuring out ways in which to live without his wife having to work, or for him to have to work full-time. Sylvia said we should try to help by picking up a place for him here. I told him that if he would give us money we would buy places here with the contingency that they give us the downpayment, and we will manage and maintain them. Anything we buy, any fix-up we do (new wallpaper, painting, etc.) we will do it at our expense, contingent that upon 5 years from when he completes his school we purchase it back from him for what he gave as a downpayment and whatever principal he paid down on it. So we did that, so he now has four places that we picked up for him for less than $25,000. He has $1160.00 a month coming in. This allows him to not have to work more than 15 hours a week running a computer lab at the university, and his wife doesn't have to work.

We were so happy about how much we were making on our first rental property. Next we went to a house auction. Actually we had a little tiff about it because Sylvia didn't think we had enough money to invest. So I went to the auction by myself. The auction was supposed to start at 10:00 A.M. and when I got there the only other people were the auctioneer and the owners.

Q: I'VE NEVER GONE TO AN AUCTION BECAUSE I FIGURED THEY WERE ALWAYS CROWDED.

A: Well, I'll tell you, I've never been to one like this one since!

Q: IT WAS JUST SUPPOSED TO BE!

A: It was just the house — no furniture — I said is this it? They said yeah — and I said this is a nice, nice little house. I ran back to our house and told Sylvia that she had to come take a look at this house. We only had one couple bidding against us (and I think they were an owner's shill) and they bid $13,500, and we bid $14,000 and we got it.

Q: AT AN AUCTION, DO YOU HAVE TO COME UP WITH THE MONEY RIGHT THEN?

A: You have to put 20% down and as soon as the abstract is done you have to come up with the remainder of the money. It usually takes about 10 days to two weeks. Some auctioneers require 20% down — some only require 10% down. It can take as much as 45 days to close actually. So we bought the house and turned right around and rented it for $350.00 just like that. The key to this whole thing is an amortizing calculator. I was in an accident a few years back and got burnt real bad. While I was recuperating I took a real estate course, which is where I learned about the amortizing calculator.

Let's say we rent it for $375.00 a month — taxes are $40.00 a month, so I subtract $40.00 — insurance is $12.00 a month, so I subtract $12.00 — on this rental the occupant pays the utilities — this is a KEY THING when you are investing in rental property, you'll want the renter to pay at least part of the utilities. If you're in a multiple building it's another story. If they can't get their electricity in their own names (not in anyone else's name) this provides you with a credit check on your potential investor.

Anyway, what we have now on this rental property is $323.00 month. You take this net amount times 12 to get how much your net is per year. In this case it's $3,876.00 — this gives us our income for the year. Then we divide this figure by what we paid for the property, which was $14,000 and you come up with our return on invested dollar, which in this case is 28%. And that's if you pay cash — and you never want to pay cash. Now you want to hear the goody? This woman I married is one smart cookie! She was CEO of a manufacturing company. So she knows what she's doing.

Now we go to our bank and ask them if they will loan us some money on this property, and they say they will go 60%, which in this case was $8,400.00. So then what we have invested in this is $5,600.00. Here's where it gets good. This is why people sometimes don't know how to play the game. So now we have $323.00 a month minus our payment on the loan of $147.00, so we get $176.00 a month net and we take that times 12, which is $2,112.00 and divide that by $5,600 and we get 38%.

Q: YOU'RE MAKING MORE MONEY ON THE PROPERTY AFTER YOU BORROWED MONEY?

A: Oh yeah, plus you're writing the interest off, which gives you even more. We haven't even taken into account that you get depreciation on the taxes. This is a business — and you have to do it professionally. I met one of our next-door neighbors, who had purchased a property and didn't even know what his return on investment was. There are too many people buying properties and not fully understanding how they can profit from it. You won't make 38% on many types of investment.

It gets better still — our bank called us and said that they had a repo - a duplex it was, in very bad condition. Three years previously it sold for $46,000 — got repossessed again and sold for $36,000 — and now the bank didn't know what to do with it. We did a walk through on it. I always take a notebook with me and make notes on EVERYTHING that needs to be done. So I did my own list on this repo, and I told our bank rep that prior to renting it it would take a minimum of $12,500 to bring it up to code. I told her you could buy a good duplex anywhere in town for the low $20,000's right now, so I told her I wouldn't give her more than $10,000 for it. She kind of gulped and said she would have to pass it by the loan committee. I told her that we didn't have much capital right now because we had been investing in properties so heavily — so we wouldn't have the capital to fix it up — so I asked her if they would sell us the house and give us the money to fix it up as part of the loan. The mortgage would cover the entire amount. She talked to the loan committee. We offered $10,000 on the place with 10% down because it was a repo (this means we only had to come up with $1,000) — borrowed $12,500 to fix it up on a 20 year mortgage. I told them that the place had been vacant for months through the winter, so there was no way of knowing what condition the plumbing would be in, and she said that the bank would take care of any plumbing necessary. This ended up being two new hot water heaters and a whole bunch of plumbing. We spent almost exactly what I said we would spend to fix it up.

Now when we are thinking about buying property I go to the County Assessors office and pull the sheet on the place. It tells you how much it has sold for, when it was last sold, all of the basic information about the building, the square footage, whether the attic is finished, etc. After I get the Assessors sheet I go to the Health Department and find out exactly what they will require to make this property into a rental. With those two pieces of paper you are in a position to make an offer. You also have to have a working knowledge of what the rents are — you don't want to under-rent or over-rent.

When a house comes up for auction we drive by it. If it looks interesting, we get ahold of the auctioneer and ask him what he thinks it's going to go for. We then set up a time to take a look at the inside of the house. We contact the Health Department and have them do an inspection to list the deficiencies, which costs us $20.00. We find out things like how many outlets will need to be put in, there's some termite damage here, you'll need a new sump pump, the roof only has about two years left in it, etc. At this point we figure out that the house goes for $10,000 — we're going to have to add $5,000 more into it — and we can only get $300.00 a month rental out of it, with a net $250.00. This would only give us a 20% return, so we pass it by unless the price at auction is substantially lower. We now own 18 rental properties (35 units), some of which yield us up to 323% on our investment.

Q: YOU'RE KIDDING. YOU CAN'T MAKE THAT KIND OF MONEY ANYWHERE ELSE, CAN YOU?

A: You can't make this type of return in every area. We were very fortunate because we were in the right place at the right time. There are other towns in the Midwest where you can do it, but you have to have a feel for the town. If I had big money right now the place I would invest would be Houston. That's an area that is really turning around, and with the oil problems we're having, Houston is going to boom.

Q: DO YOU BUY MORE AT AUCTION OR THROUGH REALTORS?

A: It's about 50/50. This area has so many elderly, that when they die, their families don't want to have to come back here to worry about their properties, so they put it with an auctioneer. Your best bet is buying single family dwellings because you are more apt to get renters who stay for awhile. Your tenants pay most of the utilities, they have their own furniture so they don't want to have to be uprooted very often. Your return on you investment dollar is not as great with single family dwellings, but you have few headaches than you do with multiple family properties.

In this area you sacrifice appreciation of the property — you must keep it up to keep it rented — and you have to put up with a lot of B.S. — but we're in a very unusual market. There are no rentals available. The strangest phenomena is that the prices on single family homes and multi-plexes don't reflect the tight rental market. The prices are still depressed.

We have been doing this for almost two years, and have been taking everything we're making and putting it back into properties.

Q: HOW DOES OUR GOVERNMENT WORK WITH YOU ON THIS?

A: Well, the tax laws changed in 1986, and they are not as advantageous because your depreciation has to be over 27-1/2 years, whereas before you had some accelerated depreciation which really helped. If you're in the right market, you're going to do okay. When we look at places to buy and figure return on investment, we do not figure property appreciation as part of the return on investment. If we get some, fantastic; but we don't count on it. We're into this big time, not everyone would have to jump in as heavily. Someone who just wants to have some steady income to assist their pension could buy two or three houses, and make a decent living.

This is so ideal for retirees because here's the thing. They only allow you $7,500 to $9,000 a year of active income if you are collecting Social Security — but you can invest in real estate and make millions in inactive income and still keep your Social Security. They consider return on investment to be inactive income. The other thing is that when you are in a fix up process the IRS has some pretty tight guidelines. If you buy a property for rental income, get someone into it as soon as possible, and then any fix-up you do after that is considered expense in the year in which its incurred. If you buy a place and you put a bunch of money in it first, that has to be depreciated over the 27 year.

Because of the fact that we are doing so much decorating in these places as we go along with them, we showed a loss on rental properties last year. Up to $25,000 of inactive income may be applied against active W-2 income. Now we didn't lose $25,000, but what we did lose was applied against our income. So it benefited us tax-wise.

A: I can only reiterate, you need a good realtor, someone in the family with a good accounting sense — plus a good accountant, and an amortizing calculator so that you can figure return on investment dollars.

Q: IN GENERAL TERMS WHAT'S THE MINIMUM RETURN YOU WOULD TAKE?

A: In this area it would be 20%. In California you'd have to have 20% because land is not appreciating. There is no strong, hard, fast rule. You should start out buying one piece of property at a time initially so that yhou learn. Each piece of property teaches you something.

23.0   THE SAVINGS AND LOAN BAIL-OUT MAY BRING YOU OPPORTUNITIES TO BUY REAL ESTATE!

The RESOLUTION TRUST CORPORATION has been given the task of selling the properties from failed Savings and Loans. Their inventory as of April 30, 1990 was over 35,000 properties.

They currently publish listings of these properties, which include everything from single family dwellings to business complexes, restaurants, recreation and resort areas, retail outlets and industrial parks.

The general consensus at the moment seems to be that many of these properties are still overvalued, and that the longer you wait to make an offer, the better your chance of actually obtaining a bargain. However, you will be wise to at least approach the Resolution Trust Corporation and inquire about properties that are available in areas that interest you — so that you can comparison shop.

For those of you who are really interested in their listings, you can order a set of books (there are three volumes, for a total of 6 books) which gives you every property they are currently trying to sell. These books were just published in June of 1990 and cost $100.00 for the set (you can buy partial sets, too).

The following will give you more information about who you should contact, and how.

150

RTC REGIONS AND SITE OFFICES

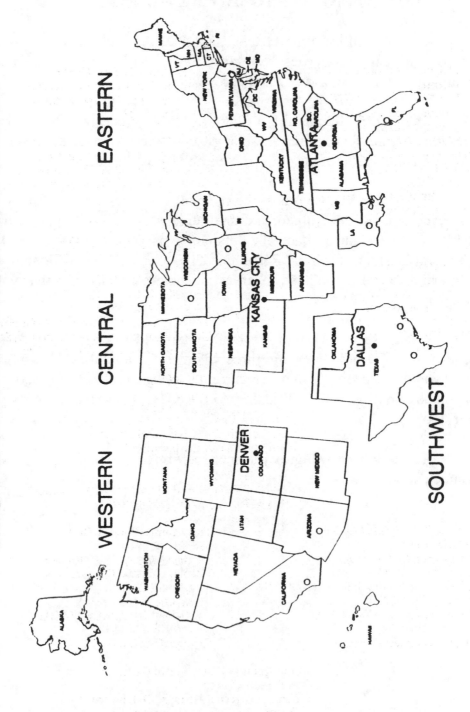

WESTERN

CENTRAL

EASTERN

SOUTHWEST

RTC Regional and Consolidated Offices

EASTERN REGION:

Atlanta Regional Office and Sales Center
Resolution Trust Corporation
Marquis One Tower, Suite 1100
243 Peachtree Center Avenue, NE
Atlanta, GA 30303
1-800-234-3342 / (404)225-5600
FAX (404)225-5004

Philadelphia Consolidated Office and Sales Center
Stephen W. Wood, C. O. Director
Resolution Trust Corporation
Valley Forge Corporate Center
1000 Adams Avenue
Norristown, PA 19403
1-800-RTCNECO / (215)650-8500
FAX:(215)650-8550
Serving: Connecticut, Delaware, Maine,
Maryland,Massachusetts, New Hamshire,
Ohio, Pennsylvania, Rhode Island,
Vermont

Northeast Satellite Office
H. Ross Ford, Director
Resolution Trust Corporation
300 Davidson Avenue
Sumerset, New Jersey 08873
1-800-542-0435
Serving: New Jersey, New York

Tampa Consolidated Office
Jimmy R. Caldwell, C.O. Director
Resolution Trust Corporation
P. O. Box 20587
Tampa, FL 33622-0587
(813)870-7000
FAX: (813) 870-7029 Contracts
FAX: (813)877-1481 Executive
Serving: Florida, Puerto Rico

Atlanta Sales Center
William C. Thomas, C. O. Director
Resolution Trust Corporation
100 Colony Sq., Suite 2300
Box 68
Atlanta, GA 30361
(404) 881-4840
FAX: (404)881-4995
Serving: Alabama, District of Columbia,
Georgia, Kentucky, North Carolina, South
Carolina, Tennessee, Virginia, West
Virginia

SOUTHWEST REGION

Dallas Regional Sales Center and Metroplex Consolidated Office
Carmen J. Sullivan, Regional Director
Resolution Trust Corporation
3500 Maple, 9th Floor
Dallas, TX 75219
1-800-782-4674 / 1-800-933-4RTC Sales Center
(214) 443-2300 / FAX: (214)969-1862

Houston Consolidated Office and Sales Center
John Lomax, C.O. Director
Resolution Trust Corporation
2223 W. Loop South, Suite 100
Houston, TX 77027
1-800-879-8492 / (713)683-3400
FAX: (713)685-3419
Serving: Southeast Texas

Tulsa Consolidated Office and Sales Center
Virginia Kingsly, C.O. Director
Resolution Trust Corporation
4606 South Garnett
Tulsa, OK 74146
1-800-456-5382 / (918)627-9000
FAX: (918)624-5803
Serving: Oklahoma

San Antonio Consolidated Office and Sales Center
James Forrestal, Acting C.O. Director
Resolution Trust Corporation
10100 Reunion Pl., Suite 250
San Antonio , TX 78216
(512)524-4749 / (512)524-4713
FAX:(512)524-7172
Serving: West Texas

152

CENTRAL REGION:

Kansas City Regional Office
Michael J. Martinelli, Regional Director
Resolution Trust Corporation
7400 W. 110th St.
Overland Park, KS 66210
1-800-283-3196 / (913)344-8100
FAX: (913)344-9360

Kansas City Regional Sales Center
Dennis Cavinaw, C.O. Director
Resolution Trust corporation
4900 Main St.
Kansas City, MO 64112
1-800-365-3342 / (816)531-2212
FAX: 9816)561-0882
Serving: Arkansas, Kansas, Missouri

**Baton Rouge Consolidated Office
and Sales Center**
Donald Wicken, C.O. Director
Resolution Trust Corporation
100 St. James Street
Suite H
Baton Rouge, LA 70802
1-800-477-8790 / (504)339-1000
FAX: (504)338-0085 REO
FAX: (504)338-0086 Contracts
FAX: (504)338-0089 Legal
Serving: Louisiana, Mississippi

**Chicago Consolidated Office
and Sales Center**
Joseph Minitti, C.O. Director
Resolution Trust Corporation
25 NW Point Boulevard
Elk Grove Village, Il 60007
1-800-526-7521
(708)806-7750
FAX: (708)290-7451
Serving: Illinois, Indiana, Michigan

**Minneapolis Consolidated Office
and Sales Center**
Robert Fish, C.O. Director
Resolution Trust Corporation
3400 Yankee Drive
Eagan, MN 55122
(612) 683-0036
FAX: (612)683-0858
Serving: Iowa, Michigan, Minnesota, South
Dakota, North Dakota, Wisconsin

WESTERN REGION:

Denver Regional Office
Anthony Scalsi, Regional Director
Resolution Trust Corporation
1225 17th Street, Suite 3200
Denver, CO 80202
1-800-283-7823 / (303)291-5700
FAX: (303)291-5906 Assets
FAX (303)291-5779 Admin.

Denver Sales Center
Keith Carson, C.O. Director
Resolution Trust Corporation
1515 Arapahoe Street
Tower 3, Suite 800
Denver, Co 80202
1-800-542-6135 / (303)556-6500
FAX: (303) 556-552 Admin.
FAX: (303) 556-6680 REO
Serving: Colordao, Idaho, Montana, New
Mexico, Utah and Wyoming

**Phoenix Consolidated Office
and Sales Center**
Dewey Porter, Director
Resolution Trust Corporation
2910 North 44th Street
Phoenix, AZ 85018
(602) 224-1776
FAX: (602) 954-9059 Admin.
Serving: Arizona, Nevada

**Costa Mesa Consolidated Office
and Sales Center**
Michael Berry, Managing Director
Resolution Trust Corporation
1901 Newport Boulevard
Costa Mesa, CA 92627
(714) 631-8600
FAX: (714) 631-8007
Serving: Arizona, California, Hawaii, Oregon, Washington, Guam

24.0 <u>IN CONCLUSION</u>

We thank you for taking the time to read this directory. We hope that you have gained a tremendous amount of knowledge that will be useful to you when buying a home.

The Appendices that follow will give you additional useful information and forms that will familiarize you with what to expect when you make a loan application.

Please let us know of your progress — and BEST OF LUCK!

The reconstruction of this house was
accomplished through Government grants.

This house was purchased as a Repo from a Savings and Loan.

APPENDICES

APPENDIX 1

THIS COULD BE YOU!!

The following are excerpts of actual recent letters from just a few of our readers who have put the information in this directory to use and who were <u>successful</u> in finding a bargain home of their own. If they could do it, then **SO CAN YOU!**

" ... It took a little while but with this book and God's help we succeeded in purchasing a beautiful old house that soon will be turned into a beautiful home for my daughter and (her) family." — N.M.P., Salem, New Jersey

"Through the use of your "How to Find a Bargain Home" book I was able to locate and buy a 3-bedroom house in a nice area for <u>nothing</u> <u>down</u> and government subsidized payments of $168.00 per month. It is part of a USDA Farmers Home project. ..." — T.R., Hope, Indiana

" ... as you mentioned, it was a little trying at times but well worth the effort! I was originally going to have to secure a regular FHA loan at 11>% but I found some bond money and am now going to get my mortgage at 9-7/8%. What a great deal! ... My new 'first' home is ... close to work and it has a beautiful back yard. It is a 2-bedroom ranch style home." — S.L.C., Kansas City, Missouri

" ... After receiving the book I started looking for property and eventually made some offers. One of the offers was accepted ... my brother and I applied for the loan through Section 221(d)(2). But that's not all. After getting the financing, we are able to rent it out for $75 per month (over and above our payments). Your publication is a real 'bible' for people who really want to own property but did not think it was possible." — P.C., Sharon Hill, Pennsylvania

" ... I am 23 years old ... having minimal savings didn't help much. Foreclosure properties seemed to be the best way for a person like myself to get a good deal on an investment property. I made about five phone calls to various mortgage companies and one had a property ready to sell. ... I saw the property that day ... and we bought the property for $32,500 ... We have the house on the market for a little over $50,000 so a substantial profit will be realized." — J.F.D., Baltimore, Maryland

WORKSHEET

This sheet is to help you keep a record of who you've contacted and what information you've received. You might first want to make copies of it for your future use.

Location & Phone No.
of my Regional HUD Office:

Program:

Who I talked to:

Program:

Who I talked to:

Program:

Who I talked to:

Location & Phone No. of my State
Housing Finance Agency/Housing Authority:

Who I talked to:

What programs did they discuss, and what was said?

Program:

Program:

LOCAL (City, County) Agencies and their Phone Numbers:

1. _____

2. _____

3. _____

4. _____

5. _____

6. _____

In the following section, write down the program you inquired about, then write down the number of the agency you just listed above so you will know who handles the program. In the larger space provided, write down information you obtained about the program, who you spoke with, etc.

Program:

Which Agency:

Comments (what they said):

Program:

Which Agency:

Comments:

Program:

Which Agency:

Comments:

NOTE: This sheet is for your records only

APPENDIX 3

HUD REPOSSESSED HOMES FOR SALE

Since many steps described in this book are up to you and can be somewhat time-consuming, we went a step further and called **every** Regional HUD office in the United States to get information about repossessed homes which they list for sale.

We asked the HUD offices how and when they advertise their repossessed homes, and who handles the sales. The responses we received are shown below — they should provide you with a great deal of helpful information, as well as save you valuable time.

An important point seemed to be that calling around to several real estate brokers in the area is a good way to get started. Not all brokers will be well-informed about the HUD repossessions, but if you don't give up after making only a few calls, you will find some that do handle these properties and who will be familiar with all the details necessary to help you.

To obtain additional information from the regional HUD offices, refer to the listing which begins on page 53.

Regional HUD Office	How and When They Advertise	Who Handles the Sales
ALABAMA **Birmingham Office**	Advertise Thursdays in *Birmingham News* *Mobile Press Register*	Call brokers
ALASKA **Anchorage Office**	Periodic ads in paper where property is located	Call brokers
ARIZONA **Indian Programs Office**	See 1100 Section of *Phoenix Republic*	1400 real estate brokers handle sales; ask if they handle HUD-acquired homes
Tucson Office	Periodic ads in *Bueno Dinero*	Call brokers; 400 in area receive listings
ARKANSAS **Little Rock Office**	No HUD advertisement List sent to brokers	Call brokers

164

CALIFORNIA
Fresno Office

No HUD advertisement
Information release
sent to brokers

Call brokers

Los Angeles Office

Every Sunday in the
L.A. Times on pg. 6 or
7 — look for ad, "HUD
Houses for Sale" with est.
prices. 10 days after ad,
sealed bids are opened.

Call brokers

San Francisco
Regional Office

Every Sunday
in *San Francisco Examiner*

Call brokers

COLORADO
Denver Regional

Sun/Mon/Wednesdays
in *Star Tribune*
Saturday/Sunday
in *Rocky Mountain News*
   Denver Post

Call brokers

CONNECTICUT
Hartford Office

Every Sunday
in *Hartford Current*
   Newhaven Register
   Bridgeport Post

Richard Weaver-Bey
343 Garden Street
Hartford CT 06112
203/522-1263

Joseph Madden
384 Whalley Avenue
New Haven CT 06508
203/776-6673
203/775-8248

DELAWARE
Wilmington

Advertise Sundays
in *Philadephia Enquirer*
Philadelphia office has
new list for Delaware
approx. every other week

Call brokers

DISTRICT OF COLUMBIA
Washington, DC
Office

Advertise Thursdays
in *WA Afro American*
At least 20 per week

Call brokers

FLORIDA
Coral Gables
Office

Friday-Saturday-Sun.
in *Miami Herald*

Call brokers

Jacksonville Office	Every Sunday in *Times-Union*	Any broker EXCEPT Watson & Co.
Orlando Office	[see Tampa Office]	
Tampa Office	Every Sunday in *Tampa Tribune* *Orlando Sentinal*	Call brokers
GEORGIA **Atlanta Regional Office**	Advertise Thursdays in *The Constitution* *Atlanta Journal*	Call brokers
HAWAII **Honolulu Office**	Usually once a month, when list available. Advertise Sundays in *Star Bulletin* *Hao-Advertiser* *Hao-Phillipine News*	Call brokers
IDAHO **Boise Office**	Advertise Sundays in *Statesman*, and on Wednesdays/Thursdays in *Advertiser*	Call brokers
ILLINOIS **Chicago Regional Office**	Every 3-4 weeks — usually every other Monday (list/book distributed to brokers)	Call brokers
Springfield Office	List sent every 3 weeks to brokers	Any broker
INDIANA **Indianapolis Office**	Advertise Sundays in *The Star*	Call brokers
IOWA **Des Moines Office**	Ads periodically on Fridays/Sundays	Call brokers
KANSAS **Topeka Office**	(see Kansas City Reg. Office)	
KENTUCKY **Louisville Office**	Every Sunday in *Louisville Courier-Journal*	Call brokers

166

LOUISIANA		
New Orleans Office	Public information release on 1st or 2nd Friday of each month	Call brokers
Shreveport Office	Every Friday in *Times-Journal* *Daily Town Talk* (Alexandria) *News Star* (Monroe) *Morning News* (Monroe)	Call brokers
MAINE	(see New Hampshire)	
MARYLAND		
Baltimore Office	Wednesdays in the *Baltimore City Paper*; Fridays in *Afro*; Sundays in *Sunday Sun*	Any broker can handle, OR call broker whose name appears on sign at property location
MASSACHUSETTS		
Boston Regional Office	Every 2 weeks in *Sunday Globe*	Too many agencies to mention
MICHIGAN		
Detroit Office	Every other Sunday in *Detroit News* *Free Press*	Call brokers
Flint Office	Advertise Sundays in *Flint Journal*	Call brokers
Grand Rapids Office	Advertise Mondays in *Grand Rapids Press*	Call brokers
MINNESOTA		
Minneapolis-St. Paul Office	Every two weeks in *Minneapolis Tribune* *St. Paul Dispatch* *Deluth News-Tribune*	Call brokers
MISSISSIPPI		
Jackson Office	No regular ads. List sent to brokers	Call brokers
MISSOURI		
Kansas City Regional Office	Advertise Sundays in *Kansas City Star*	Call brokers

St. Louis Office	Every Sunday in *Post Dispatch*	Call brokers
MONTANA **Helena Office**	No HUD advertisement List sent to brokers	Call brokers
NEBRASKA **Omaha Office**	Every Monday in *World Herald*	Call brokers
NEVADA **Las Vegas Office**	Every Saturday/Sunday in *Las Vegas Sun* *Review-Journal*	Call brokers
NEW HAMPSHIRE **Manchester Offc**	(Maine, Vermont, New Hampshire)	Call brokers
NEW JERSEY **Camden Office**	Every Friday (all listings) in the *Camden Courier-Post*	Most brokers handle the sales
Newark Office	Every Sunday in real estate section in *Asbury Park Press* *Newark Star Ledger* *Home News*	Call licensed brokers
NEW MEXICO **Albuquerque Office**	Sundays when avail. in *Albuquerque Journal*	Call brokers
NEW YORK **Albany Office**	Blanket ad (no specifics) when property available in *Impartial Citizen*	Call Albany office for list of brokers in area of interest
Buffalo Office	Every Friday in *Buffalo Evng News* In Rochester, in *Democratic* *Chronicle* *Times-Union*	Any broker registered with HUD

New York
Regional Office
	Every Friday
	in *Daily News*
	   News Day
	   Amsterdam News
		Call brokers

NORTH CAROLINA **Greensboro Office**	No HUD advertisement List goes to brokers	Creeksman Realty Patton Realty MT & Associates
NORTH DAKOTA **Fargo Office**	Advertise Sundays in *Fargo Forum*	Call brokers

OHIO
Cincinnati Office
	Advertise Thursdays
	in *Cincinnati Post*
	Advertise Fridays
	in *Cincinnati Enquirer*
	   Cincinnati Herald
	   Dayton Daily News
		Call brokers

Cleveland Office	Every other Monday in *Cleveland Plain Dealer*	Call brokers
Columbus Office	Advertise Sundays in *Columbus Dispatch*	Call brokers
OKLAHOMA **Oklahoma City** **Office**	Advertise Saturdays in *Saturday Oklahoman*	Call brokers
Tulsa Office	Advertise Sundays in *Tulsa World* and during the week in *Oklahoma Eagle*	Call brokers
OREGON **Portland Office**	Advertise Fridays in *The Oregonian*	Call brokers; if agent not currently on list, they can call HUD for info & key to property
PENNSYLVANIA **Philadelphia** **Regional Office**	Every Sunday in *Enquirer*	Lambs Real Estate 2979 Frankford Ave No. Philadelphia PA 739-4339

Pennsylvania (cont'd)		Joseph Austin R.E. 3140 Front Street Philadelphia PA GA5-3388
		(There are others, call around)
Pittsburgh Office	Occasionally on Fri-Sat-Sun in *The Press*	Call brokers
RHODE ISLAND **Providence Offc**	Advertise, when property available, in *Providence Journal*	Call brokers
SOUTH CAROLINA **Columbia Office**	Advertise when list is available in diff. papers across state (where property located)	Call brokers
SOUTH DAKOTA **Sioux Falls Office**	(see Denver Reg. Office)	
TENNESSEE **Knoxville Office**	Every Tuesday in *Knoxville Journal* *Knoxville News-Sentinal*	Call brokers
Memphis Office	Every Sunday in *Commercial Appeal*	Call brokers
Nashville Office	Every Sunday in *The Tennessean*	Call brokers
TEXAS **Dallas Office**	[see Forth Worth Office]	
Ft. Worth **Office**	Every Friday in *Star Telegram* *Times-Herald* (Dallas)	Call brokers
Houston Office	Every Friday in *Houston Chronicle* *Houston Post*	20 brokers listed near advertisement in paper
San Antonio Office	Periodical public information release	850 brokers on HUD mailing list — call

170

UTAH **Salt Lake City** **Office**	Advertise Sundays in *Deseret News* *Salt Lake Tribune*	Call brokers
VERMONT	(see New Hampshire)	
VIRGINIA **Richmond Office**	Periodically adver- tise by area management brokers	800+ brokers in area with listings (call around)
WASHINGTON **Seattle Regional** **Office**	Every Wednesday in *Seattle P.I.* Some Sundays in <u>Seattle Times</u>	Call brokers
Spokane Office	Alternate weekly ads in *Tri-City Herald* & *Spokesman Review*	Kennewick/Spokane realty members receive HUD lists
WEST VIRGINIA **Charleston Office**	Sundays in the *Charleston Gazette*	Call for list of brokers; 600+, 20 out-of-state
WISCONSIN **Milwaukee Office**	Every Friday in *Milwaukee Journal*	Call brokers
WYOMING **Casper Office**	(see Denver Reg. Office)	
PUERTO RICO **Caribbean Office**	Every Friday in *Nuevo Dia* *El Mundo* *El Vocero*	Newspaper gives listing of brokers/ addresses who handle the sales

APPENDIX 4

GLOSSARY OF REAL ESTATE TERMS

ABSTRACT: A short legal history of a piece of property, tracing its ownership (title) through the years. An attorney or title insurance company reviews the abstract to make sure the title comes to a buyer free from any defects (problems).

ACCELERATION CLAUSE: A provision in a mortgage which may require the unpaid balance of the mortgage loan to become due immediately if the regular mortgage payments are not made, or if other terms of the mortgage are not met.

AGREEMENT OF SALE: (see Purchase Agreement)

AMORTIZATION: A payment plan by which the borrower reduces his debt gradually through monthly payments of principal.

APPRECIATION: An increase in the value of property.

APPRAISAL: An evaluation of a piece of property to determine its value; that is, what it would sell for in the marketplace.

ASSESSMENT: The value placed on property for purposes of taxation; may also refer to a special tax due for a special purpose, such as a sewer assessment.

ASSUMPTION OF MORTGAGE: The promise by the buyer of property to be legally responsible for the payment of an existing mortgage. The purchaser's name is substituted for the original mortgagor's (borrower's) name on the mortgage note and the original mortgagor is released from the responsibility of making the mortgage payments. Usually the lender must agree to an assumption.

BINDER: A simple contract between a buyer and a seller which states the basic terms of an offer to purchase property. It is usually good only for a limited period of time, until a more formal purchase agreement is prepared and signed by both parties. A small deposit of earnest money is made to "bind" the offer.

BROKER: (see Real Estate Broker)

172

CERTIFICATE OF TITLE: A document prepared by a title company or an attorney stating that the seller has a clear, marketable and insurable title to the property he is offering for sale.

CLOSING: The final step in the sale and purchase of a property, when the title is transferred from the seller to the buyer; the buyer signs the mortgage, pays settlement costs; and any money due the seller or buyer is handed over.

CLOSING COSTS: Sometimes called Settlement Costs — costs in addition to the price of a house, usually including mortgage origination fee, title insurance, attorney's fee, and prepayable items such as taxes and insurance payments collected in advance and held in an escrow account.

CLOUD ON TITLE: (see Title Defect)

COMMISSION: Money paid to a real estate agent or broker by the seller as payment for finding a buyer and completing a sale. Usually it is a percentage of the sales price and is spelled out in the purchase agreement.

COMMUNITY PROPERTY: In some states, a form of ownership under which property acquired during a marriage is presumed to be owned jointly unless acquired as separate property of either spouse.

CONDITIONAL COMMITMENT: A promise to insure (generally with FHA loans) payment of a definite loan amount on a particular piece of property for a buyer with satisfactory credit.

CONDOMINIUM: Individual ownership of an apartment in a multi-unit project or development, and a proportionate interest in the common areas outside the apartment.

CONTRACTOR: A person or company who agrees to furnish materials and labor to do work for a certain price.

CONVENTIONAL LOAN: A mortgage loan which is not insured by FHA or guaranteed by VA.

COOPERATIVE: An apartment building or group of housing units owned by all the residents (generally a corporation) and run by an elected board of directors for the benefit of the residents. The resident lives in his unit but does not own it — he owns a share of stock in the corporation.

CREDIT RATING: A rating or evaluation made by a person or company (such as a Credit Bureau) based on one's present financial condition and past credit history.

CREDIT REPORT: A report usually ordered by a lender from a credit bureau to help determine a borrower's credit rating.

DEED: A written document by which the ownership of property is transferred from the seller (the grantor) to the buyer (the grantee).

DEED OF TRUST: In some states, a document used instead of a mortgage. It transfers title of the property to a third party (the trustee) who holds the title until the debt or mortgage loan is paid off, at which time the title (ownership) passes to the borrower. If the borrower defaults (fails to make payments), the trustee may sell the property at a public sale to pay off the loan.

QUITCLAIM DEED: A deed which transfers only that title or right to a property that the holder of that title has at the time of the transfer. A quitclaim deed does not warrant (or guarantee) a clear title.

WARRANTY DEED: A deed which guarantees that the title to a piece of property is free from any title defects.

DEFAULT: Failure to make mortgage payments on time, as agreed to in the mortgage note or deed of trust. If a payment is 30 days late, the mortgage is in default, and it may give the lender the right to start foreclosure proceedings.

DELINQUENCY: When a mortgage payment is past due.

DEPOSIT: A sum of money given to bind a sale of real estate — also called earnest money.

DEPRECIATION: A loss or decrease in the value of a piece of property due to age, wear and tear, or unfavorable changes in the neighborhood; opposite of appreciation.

DOCUMENTARY STAMPS: In some states, a tax in the form of stamps, required on deeds and mortgages when real estate title passes from one owner to another. The amount required differs from one state to another.

174

EARNEST MONEY: (see Deposit)

EASEMENT: The right to use land owned by another. For instance, the electric company has easement rights to allow their power lines to cross another's property.

ECOA: Equal Credit Opportunity Act — a federal law that requires lenders to loan without discrimination based on race, color, religion, national origin, sex, marital status, or income from public assistance programs.

ENCUMBRANCE: Anything that limits the interest in a title to property such as a mortgage, a lien, an easement, a deed restriction or unpaid taxes.

EQUITY: A buyer's initial ownership interest in a house that increases as he pays off a mortgage loan. When the mortgage is fully paid, the owner has 100% equity in his house.

ESCROW: Money or documents held by a third party until all the conditions of a contract are met.

ESCROW AGENT: The third party responsible to the buyer and seller or to the lender and borrower for holding the money or documents until the terms of a purchase agreement are met.

ESCROW PAYMENT: That part of a borrower's monthly payment held by the lender to pay for taxes, hazard insurance, mortgage insurance, and other items until they become due. Also known as impounds or reserves in some states.

FHA: Federal Housing Administration — a division of the U.S. Department of Housing and Urban Development (HUD). Its main activity is to insure home mortgage loans made by private lenders.

FmHA: Farmers Home Administration — a government agency (part of the Dept of Agriculture) which provides financing to farmers or other qualified buyers (usually in rural areas who are unable to obtain loans elsewhere.

FINANCE CHARGE: The total of all charges one must pay in order to get a loan.

FIRM COMMITMENT: An agreement from a lender to make a loan to a particular borrower on a particular property. Also an FHA or private mortgage insurance company agreement to insure a loan on a particular property for a particular borrower.

FOREBEARANCE: The act of delaying legal action to foreclose on a mortgage that is overdue. Usually it is granted only when a satisfactory arrangement has been made with the lender to make up the late payments at a future date.

FORECLOSURE: The legal process by which a lender forces payment of a loan (under a mortgage or deed of trust) by taking the property from the owner (mortgagor) and selling it to pay off the debt.

GRANTEE: That party in the deed who is the buyer.

GRANTOR: That party in the deed who is the seller.

GUARANTEED LOAN: A loan guaranteed to be paid by the VA or FmHA in the event the borrower fails to do so (defaults).

GUARANTY: A promise by one party to pay the debt of another if that other fails to do so.

HAZARD INSURANCE: Insurance which protects against damage caused to property by fire, windstorm, or other common hazard. Required by many lenders to be carried in an amount at least equal to the mortgage.

HOMEOWNERS INSURANCE POLICY: Insurance that covers the house and its contents in the case of fire, wind damage, theft, and covers the homeowner in case someone is injured on the property and brings a suit.

HUD: The U.S. Department of Housing and Urban Development.

IMPOUND: (see Escrow)

INSTALLMENT: The regular payment that a borrower agrees to make to a lender.

INSURANCE BINDER: A document stating that an individual or property is insured, even though the insurance policy has not yet been issued.

INSURED LOAN: A loan insured by FHA or a private mortgage insurance company.

INTEREST:	A charge paid for borrowing money. Also a right, share or title in property.
JOINT TENANCY:	An equal, undivided ownership of property by two or more persons. Should one of the parties die, his share of the ownership would pass to the surviving owners (right of survivorship).
LATE CHARGE:	An additional fee a lender charges a borrower if his mortgage payments are not made on time.
LIEN:	A hold or claim which someone has on the property of another, as security for a debt or charge; if a lien is not removed (if a debt is not paid), the property may be sold to pay off the lien.
LISTING:	Registering of properties for sale with one or more real estate brokers or agents allowing the broker who actually sells the property to get the commission.
LOAN DISCLOSURE NOTE:	Document spelling out all the terms involved in obtaining and paying off a loan.
MORTGAGE:	A special loan for buying property.
MORTGAGE INTEREST SUBSIDY:	A monthly payment by the Federal Government to a mortgagee (lender) which reduces the amount of interest the mortgagor (homeowner) has to pay to the lender to as low as 4%, if the homeowner falls within certain income limits.
MORTGAGE ORIGINATION FEE:	A charge by the lender for the work involved in the preparation and servicing of a mortgage request. Usually 1% of the loan amount.
MORTGAGEE:	The lender who makes a mortgage loan.
MORTGAGOR:	The person borrowing money for a mortgage loan.
OPTION (TO BUY):	An agreement granting a potential buyer the right to buy a piece of property at a stated period of time.
PITI:	Principal, interest, taxes and insurance (in FHA and VA loans paid to the bank each month).

**PLAT
(or PLOT):** A map of a piece of land showing its boundaries, length, width, and any easements.

POINT(S): An amount equal to 1% of the principal amount of a loan. Points are a one-time charge collected by the lender at closing to increase the return on the loan. In FHA or VA loans, the borrower is not allowed to pay any points.

**PREPAID
ITEMS:** An advance payment, at the time of closing, for taxes, hazard insurance and mortgage insurance which is held in an escrow account by the lender.

**PREPAYMENT
PENALTY:** A charge made by the lender if a mortgage loan is paid off before the due date. FHA does not permit such a penalty on its FHA-insured loans.

PRINCIPAL: The amount of money borrowed which must be paid back, along with interest and other finance charges.

**PURCHASE
AGREEMENT:** A written document in which a seller agrees to sell, and a buyer agrees to buy a piece of property, with certain conditions and terms of the sale spelled out, such as sales price, date of closing, condition of property, etc. The agreement is secured by a deposit or down payment of earnest money.

REAL ESTATE: Land and the structures thereon. Also anything of a permanent nature such as trees, minerals, and the interest and rights in these items.

**REAL ESTATE
AGENT:** An individual who can show property for sale on behalf of a seller, but who may not have a license to transact the sale and collect the sales commission.

**REAL ESTATE
BROKER:** An individual who can show property for sale on behalf of a seller, and who has a valid license to sell real estate. The real estate broker represents the seller and is paid a commission when the property is sold.

REALTOR: A real estate broker or an associate holding active membership in a local real estate board affiliated with the National Association of Realtors.

RECORDING

178

FEES:	The charge by an attorney to put on public record the details of legal documents such as a deed or mortgage.
REFINANCING:	The process of paying off one loan with the money (proceeds) from another loan.
RESPA:	Real Estate Settlement Procedures Act — a federal law that requires lenders to send to the home mortgage borrower (within 3 business days) an estimate of closing (settlement) costs. RESPA also limits the amount lenders may hold in an escrow account for real estate taxes and insurance, and requires the disclosure of settlement costs to both buyers and sellers 24 hours before the closing.
RESTRICTIONS:	A legal limitation in the deed on the use of property.
RIGHT OF RECISSION:	That section of the Truth-in-Lending Law which allows a consumer the right to change his/her mind and cancel a contract within 3 days after signing it. This right to cancel is in force if the contract would involve obtaining a loan, and the loan would place a lien on the property.
RIGHT OF WAY:	An easement on property, where the property owner gives another person the right to pass over his land.
SALES AGREEMENT:	(see Purchase Agreement)
SETTLEMENT COSTS:	(see Closing Costs)
SOLE OWNER:	Ownership of a property by a single individual.
SURVEY:	A map or plat made by a licensed surveyor showing the measurements of a piece of land; its location, dimensions, and the location and dimensions of any improvements on the land.
TENANCY-BY-THE-ENTIRETY:	The joint ownership of property by a husband and wife. If either one dies, his or her share of ownership goes to the survivor.
TENANCY-IN-COMMON:	When property is owned by two or more persons with the terms creating a joint tenancy. In the event one of the owners dies, his share of the property would not go to the other automatically, but rather to his heirs.

TITLE: The rights of ownership of a particular property, and the documents which prove that ownership (commonly a deed)

TITLE DEFECTS: An outstanding claim or encumbrance on property which affects its marketability (whether or not it can be freely sold).

TITLE INSURANCE: Special insurance which usually protects lenders against loss of their interest in property due to legal defects in the title. An owner can protect his interest by purchasing separate coverage.

TITLE SEARCH: An examination of public records to uncover any past or current facts regarding the ownership of a piece of property. A title search is intended to make sure the title is marketable and free from defects.

TRUTH-IN-LENDING: A federal law which provides that the terms of a loan (including all the finance charges) must be disclosed to the borrower before the loan is signed. It also contains a provision for the Right of Recission.

VA: Veterans Administration — The VA guarantees a certain proportion of a mortgage loan made to a veteran by a private lender. Sometimes called GI loans, these usually require very low down payment and permit long repayment terms.

ZONING: The power of a local municipal government (city or town) to regulate the use of property within the municipality.

APPENDIX 5

EXAMPLE OF WHY IT IS NECESSARY TO CALL

EVERY LENDER ON THE LIST

Just to demonstrate how important it is that you CALL EVERY SINGLE LENDER, I sat down and called a list of lenders here in my own city to ask about their regular (non-HUD) home mortgages. I suggest that it will be less confusing to you, when trying to compare rates of the different programs offered, to just **take one program at a time** and go through the list of lenders completely, asking only about that one program. When you have received the answers to that program, go through the list of lenders the next day and ask questions about the next program you are interested in. This won't take nearly as long as you might imagine. For one thing, not all lenders handle HUD-insured loans. For another thing, not all the lenders which handle HUD-insured loans handle <u>every</u> type of loan. And lastly, the government insured loans will be very specific as far as interest rates, amounts allowed, etc., so there won't be as many variables as with a private loan.

This list of calls took me just 45 minutes, and I think you'll agree it is a valuable cache of information to have at my hands. Even though making the calls may be somewhat tedious, just tell yourself that you have been hired by someone who is paying you very well and you only have to do it for one hour. You <u>are</u> being paid well to do it -- look at the difference you would pay between one loan and another. So you simply can't afford to make only one or two calls before getting your home loan. Call them **all**!

I have used numbers instead of names of companies, as the names are not necessary for the purposes of this example. I called each of these companies and asked the same question: WHAT INTEREST RATE DO YOU HAVE FOR A $100,000 HOME LOAN ON A 30-YEAR FIXED RATE? Here are the answers (check the Glossary on page 118 for terms you are unfamiliar with):

1. 9-7/8% plus 3 points, or 10% plus 2-1/2 points

2. 10-3/8% plus 1 point

3. Phone number changed, no answer at new number

4. They don't do first mortgages

5. On hold for a long time; 12-3/4% amortized over 30 years, but due in 10 years

6. Number changed, person will call back

7. Number changed, new number disconnected

182

8. 10-3/4%, plus 1 point, plus $200; or
10-1/2%, plus 2-1/4 points, plus $200; or
10-1/4%, plus 3-1/2 points, plus $200

9. Will call back

10. 11.95% due in 15 years

11. 11% or 12%, due in 5 years

12. They don't do first mortgages

13. Passed through 3 people, then told they don't do firsts

14. Don't do long-term loans

15. 10-1/4%, plus 2 points, plus you have to buy 6% stock in the bank
(which is refundable when you pay off the loan completely)

16. With 20% down payment, 11-1/4%, plus 4 points, plus $300; with 10%
down, 11-1/2%, plus 5 points, plus $300

17. They called back and said 10-1/8%, plus 2 points, plus $250

18. Will call back

19. Recording -- left message for them to call back

20. 11%, plus 1-1/2 points, plus $250

21. 10.75%, plus 2 points, plus $200

22. They don't do long-term loans

23. Number changed, new number busy

24. Will call back "tomorrow or next day"

25. 10-1/4%, plus 3 points, plus $200; or
10-1/2%, plus 2 points, plus $200; or
10-3/4%, plus 1 point, plus $200

26. No fixed rates -- all Adjustable Rate Mortgages

27. $75,000 is their maximum loan amount

28. 10.875%, plus 1 point, plus $200;
10.75%, plus 1 point, plus $200
10.50%, plus 1.25 points, plus $200
10.25%, plus 2.25 points, plus $200

10.00%, plus 3.25 points, plus $200
9.75%, plus 5.25 points, plus $200
9.50%, plus 7.25 points, plus $200

Now let's compare what your payments per month would be and the total amount of interest you would pay over the years with several of these mortgages:

(A)   **11.50% (30-year loan), plus 7.25 points, plus $200:**

Initial cost of $7,250 (points) plus $200
Payments would be $980.89 per month
$253,124.06 total interest paid after 30 years

(B)   **12.125% (30-year loan), plus 2 points, plus $250:**

Initial cost of $2,000 (points) plus $250
Payments would be $1,027.86 per month
$270,025.30 total interest paid after 30 years

APPENDIX 6

YOUR DAILY NEWSPAPER: A VALUABLE SOURCE

If you're like most people, you have trouble getting started because you're not really sure where to look to find the housing programs. One of the most valuable sources of information you have comes to your doorstep every day — your daily newspaper! Not only does it carry many ads from the various housing agencies, but don't forget that in the "Public Notices" section, repossession sales are listed, among other housing opportunities. Be sure to look through **every page** when you decide to seriously look for a home.

Still, unless you have seen actual samples of an agency's ad, you could be browsing through your paper and actually miss an ad that's exactly what you are looking for. That's why we've accumulated several ads and articles to show you: the next few pages are full of the type of thing you should be looking for.

Get out your newspaper and start looking for these types of articles and ads:

186

It's easy to own a single family home when you buy from HUD.

Right now, you can purchase a single family home at an attractive price from the United States Government. Just contact your local real estate broker who will explain the details of the sale and process your bid application at no cost to you.

Now's the time to buy a single family home ... from HUD. **Contact your local realtor today.**

 HUD DEPARTMENT OF HOUSING AND URBAN DEVELOPMENT

Home Rehabilitation Loans Now Available

For a limited time, the Community Development Commission of the County of Los Angeles, has funds available to qualified property owners in the County unincorporated areas for low interest home improvement loans. Loans up to $27,000 may be made with a maximum repayment term of 20 years. For loans to homeowners with adjusted income of not more than 80% of the median income, the interest rate may not exceed three percent (3%) per year. The interest on loans to homeowners with adjusted income greater than 80% of the median income, will parallel but not exceed the current average market yeild rate.

County of Los Angeles Community Dev. Commission

City may issue bonds for hotel improvements

The city Redevelopment Agency may issue $3.5 million in tax-exempt bonds to finance a private plan to purchase and rehabilitate the New Carrillo Retirement Hotel downtown.

The City Council has scheduled a March 5 public hearing on the bond proposal.

The Urban Group, composed of Richard W. Sanders, Maxwell Sanders, Robert E. Parsons and Allyce A. Parsons, wants to buy the 172-room hotel at 31 W. Carrillo St. and continue its operation as a facility for senior citizens.

State law permits the agency to issue the industrial development bonds to finance housing for low- to moderate-income residents or industrial-type projects that create jobs or other benefits. No agency money would be involved in the project, and the bonds would be paid off by the developers.

The developers have agreed to make 20 percent of the hotel's units available for 10 years at rents that qualify under the city Housing Authority's Section 8 rent subsidy program for low-income residents.

Some council members expressed concern that rents on the other units would be raised to pay for the improvements, forcing out some of the hotel's mostly low- and moderate-income residents.

John Bridley, city housing and redevelopment manager, said there is no guarantee that other rents won't be raised, but the developers have indicated they have no plan to change the rent structure.

At the council's request, the agency is attempting to negotiate a higher percentage of low-income units with the developers.

The developers will be required to continue the hotel's "market orientation" as a senior citizen facility, Bridley noted.

The Urban Group plans rehabilitation to improve the building's appearance and strengthen it against possible earthquake damage.

Santa Barbara News Press -- February, 1985

PUBLIC NOTICE

TO ALL INTERESTED AGENCIES, GROUPS AND CITIZENS OF THE CITY OF SANTA BARBARA:

Copies of the City of Santa Barbara's **Proposed Statement of Community Development Objectives and Proposed Use of Funds** are available for review and comment at the below listed address. The proposed statement contains a description of the use of Community Development Block Grant Entitlement Funds for FY 85 and FY's 84 & 83. It also contains an assessment of the use of funds for FY's 83-84 and how the "Maximum Feasible Priority" was addressed.

Persons residing in Census Tracts 8, 9, 10, 11 and 12.01 would have particular interest in the proposed activities. As the projects benefiting low and moderate income persons will be concentrated in these areas.

The City's plan to minimize displacement (even though the City has no intention to cause displacement) is available for review.

The City expects to receive approximately $1,033,000 in CDBG Funds. For further information, call or visit
Community Development Coordinator, City of Santa Barbara, Community Development Department.

190

City/suburbs

Abandoned homes set for lottery

By Stanley Ziemba
Urban affairs writer

The City of Chicago will hold a lottery June 1 to award 54 abandoned single-family houses for $1 each to individuals willing to repair and live in the houses.

The lottery, scheduled for noon in the Auditorium Theatre, 70 E. Congress St., will be the first under the city's urban homesteading program since 1981, when 120 houses were given out.

A person may take part in the lottery if his annual family income is at least $20,500 and not more than $36,200, depending on the number of dependents, city housing officials said. He also must show that he has financial resources to repair the house.

An applicant must be a Chicago resident, officials said.

Applications for the lottery are available at the city's Department of Housing office, 318 S. Michigan Ave.; at City Hall; and at public library branches throughout the city.

They may also be obtained from some community organizations and at aldermanic offices in each ward.

A person awarded a house will be required to move into it within 60 days of receiving a conditional deed, housing officials said.

He will have 18 months to bring the home into compliance with the city's building code and will be required to live in the house for five years before obtaining clear title to the property, according to the officials.

The abandoned houses come from the federal Department of Housing and Urban Development's inventory of repossessed homes. HUD repossesses the houses of homeowners who fail to meet monthly payments on federally insured mortgages.

The houses available are in the Austin, Pilsen, Roseland, West Englewood, West Town, Humboldt Park and South Shore communities, city housing officials said.

Since Chicago began its urban homesteading program in 1976, 425 abandoned, single-family homes have been sold to individuals for $1 each, records show. Only five of the houses have been abandoned again.

Though the urban homesteading program has restored some abandoned houses to the city's tax rolls, about 1,200 vacant single-family houses are torn down each year because their owners have not paid taxes and have allowed the houses to deteriorate.

A national housing rights group, the Association of Community Organizations for Reform Now [ACORN], is trying to heighten public awareness of the loss of such housing by having homeless people move into the abandoned houses as squatters.

The activist group's Chicago chapter Tuesday moved 10 of its members into abandoned houses in Englewood on the city's South Side and called on Chicago and Cook County officials to enact ordinances that would permit low- and moderate-income people to take possession of and repair tax-delinquent and abandoned single-family houses.

Madeline Talbott, organizer for ACORN in Chicago, said her organization is working closely with some Chicago aldermen and Cook County commissioners to come up with a program for salvaging as many vacant single-family homes as possible.

(reprinted by courtesy of the Chicago Tribune)

AUCTION

AS I HAVE SOLD MY HOME AND AM MOVING TO SMALLER HOME, I WILL SELL THE FOLLOWING AT AUCTION ON

FRIDAY, AUGUST 3, 1990
4:00 P.M.
SALE WILL BE CONDUCTED AT THE PROPERTY LOCATED

1301 S. MILNER, OTTUMWA, IOWA

<u>APPLIANCES, FURNITURE & HOUSEHOLD ITEMS:</u> Westinghouse coppertone refrigerator/freezer; Tappan coppertone gas oven & range; Montgomery Ward dehumidifier; older hardwick gas oven & range, green 3 cushion floral upholstered sofa & matching swivel rocker; square formica top dinette table w/extra leaf & 4 chairs; Maytag automatic washer & gas dryer; older cabinet model record player; antique square occasional table; floral upholstered swivel rocker; smoking stand; oil lamp; Duncan Phyfe drop leaf table & 6 matching chairs; electric sewing machine in cabinet; oak table; full size bed w/mattress & box springs, matching dresser w/large mirror & vanity bench; humidifier; 2 upholstered swivel rockers; floor & table lamps; movie screen; naugahyde upholstered platform rocker; 2 folding card tables; old baskets; ironing board; foot stool; 2 metal storage cabinets; 3 shelf serving cart; wicker plant stand; large assortment of kitchen items including toaster oven, pots, pans, electric fry pan, strainers, Tupperware, deep fat fryer, roaster, toaster, silverware & other kitchen items; Hamilton Beach platform mixer; Snapper 20" self-propelled, electric start lawnmower; 6 ft. aluminum stepladder; garden plow; sprayer; assortment of hand tools including hammers, saws, files, level, circular saw, hoes, rakes & shovels.

<u>CONSIGNED BY OTHERS:</u> 3 cushion turquoise full size sofa; near new, sleeper sofa; near new rocker recliner; humidifier; TV trays; fans; kitchen table & 6 chairs; 13" b/w TV; Tappan microwave; microwave stand; full size bed w/dresser & 2 night stands; trunks; pictures & frames; typewriter; stereo; record stand; recliner; exercise bike; china hutch; 5,000 BTU window air conditioner; assortment of bedding, linens, towels & material.

TERMS-CASH   POSITIVE ID REQUIRED

MRS. FREIDA HENNESS, OWNER

All property must be settled for before removal. Not responsible in case of accidents.
Announcements made day of sale take precedence over any advertising.

SALE CONDUCTED BY

AL MARTIN REAL ESTATE & AUCTION CO.

PHONE: 682-5465   819 CHURCH ST.

192

AUCTION

AS I AM NO LONGER ABLE TO MAINTAIN MY HOME, I WILL SELL THE FOLLOWING ON

SUN. AUG. 5, 12 NOON

SALE WILL BE CONDUCTED AT THE PROPERTY LOCATED

1303 E. MAIN, OTTUMWA, IA

REAL ESTATE

Real estate consists of an older, neat, clean, 4 room, 2 bedroom home with large living room/dining room, 2 spacious bedrooms, full bath, ample size kitchen with eating area. This home has aluminum siding on the exterior with full basement and gas forced air heat. This home is nicely decorated throughout with new carpeting, recently painted on the interior and is ready to move into. Dwelling is located on a corner lot measuring 49 feet wide by 130 feet in depth. Also located on the property is an older, 16X20 detached garage.

TERMS: 20% down day of sale, balance in cash upon delivery of a Warranty Deed accompanied by Abstract of Title showing merchantable title. Real estate taxes will be pro-rated to possession date, possession given upon settlement.

REAL ESTATE WILL SELL AT 1:00 P.M.

For further particulars or appointment to inspect the property, please call the auction company.

APPLIANCES, FURNITURE & HOUSEHOLD ITEMS: GE no frost refrigerator/freezer; Hardwick gas double oven & range; GE automatic washer & matching electric dryer; RCA 19" portable color TV w/remote, less than 2 years old; wooden & chrome dinette table w/glass top & 4 matching chairs, like new; 2 brown velour upholstered swivel rockers, like new; 3 piece bedroom suite including full size bed, mattress & box springs; dresser w/mirror & 4 drawer chest; Lane cedar chest; old square trunk, like new, brown upholstered 2 cushion hide-a-bed sofa; glass top; mahogany coffe table & matching step end table; foot stool; assortment of pictures & frames; clock radio; 4 shelf metal book shelf; cedar lined wardrobe; kitchen step stool; Electrolux sweeper w/attachments; metal porch glider; metal lawn chairs; luggage; old cabinet radio; 3 piece bedroom suite, full size bed, mattress & box springs; dresser w/large mirror & 4 drawer chest; ironing board; wooden armed, upholstered straight chair; telephone stand; cuckoo clock, like new; fruitwood corner hutch w/glass doors; small microwave oven; large assortment of pots; pans; dishes; & kitchen items including coffee maker; crock pot; toaster oven; deep fat fryer; Mr. Coffee; pressure canner; silverware; Tupperware & Pyrex & other kitchen items; bedding; linens; rugs; towels; assortment of Christmas decorations; plant stand; whatnot shelf; 12 ft. wooden straight ladder; assortment of lawn & garden tools including hoes; rakes; shovels; garden hose & other items.

TERMS--CASH POSITIVE ID REQUIRED

MINNIE V. PUTMAN, OWNER

Edna Meeker, POA   Box & Box Attorneys

All property must be settled for before removal.
Not responsible in case of accidents.
Announcments made day of sale take precedence over any advertising.

SALE CONDUCTED BY

AL MARTIN REAL ESTATE & AUCTION CO.

Ph. 682-5465   819 Church St.

193

EXAMPLE OF LOCAL GOVERNMENT SUBSIDIZED HOUSING AD

LA COLINA VILLAGE
AFFORDABLE CONDOMINIUMS

**Charming New England townhouses
Sunny southern exposure
Energy-saving passive solar design
Private fenced yards
2 and 3 bedrooms
Utility room
Energy-efficient built-in kitchen
Wall-to-wall carpeting & drapes**

Below-market financing is available for these 50 condominiums. Apply before January 31 for June occupancy.

Please call

**Equal Housing
Opportunity**

**Developed by
Santa Barbara Community
Housing Corporation.**

Look for these indications of government programs

APPENDIX 7

AN IDEA THAT MAKES FINANCIAL SENSE

(PREPAY A SMALL AMOUNT OF THE PRINCIPAL ON YOUR HOME MORTGAGE EACH MONTH)
or

HOW $3,240 CAN SAVE YOU $15,426!

Have you ever given any thought to how much money that interest rate on your loan actually amounts to? Well, an innocent sounding little 12% can really add up over the years. And the longer the length of your mortgage, the more interest you pay in the end. Have you ever heard someone say that they have been making payments on their house loan for years and _still_ owe the full amount of the original loan? Let's take a look at why that is:

Say you took out a loan for *$10,000 at 12% interest for 30 years*. Your payments would be $102.80 per month. If you paid it off in 30 years, you would have paid $27,029.60 just in interest, plus the $10,000 you originally borrowed. If you paid it off in 15 years, making payments of $120.02 per month, you would pay a total of $11,603.60 in interest, plus the $10,000 you borrowed. So, if you get the loan approved for 30 years, but each month pay an extra $18 (the difference in payment amounts between the 15-year amortization schedule and the 30-year schedule) and ask that the extra payment be applied to the principal, not only would you pay off the loan in half the time, but *YOU WOULD HAVE SAVED YOURSELF $15,426.00*. In the 15 years you would have paid out $3,240 ($18 per month) in principal, and that would cause you to save $15,426.00 in interest (the difference between the total interest you would have paid if the loan had run out the full 30 years = $27,029.60 less the total interest you will have paid by paying it off in 15 years = $11,603.60).

$27,029.60
- 11,603.60
$15,426.00 =   YOUR SAVINGS. Your investment
of $18/month will mean a return
of over **500%** on your money!

Yes, this is completely legal. Just be sure to check your loan papers and see that they don't say "PENALTY FOR EARLY REPAYMENT" — most do not, especially the government loans. Not only is this legal and **extremely** beneficial to you, but your banker will love it, too. He can use that money to lend out to someone else — probably at a higher rate of interest — if you pay it off early. And paying off a loan early looks absolutely **great** on your credit record. This is the most win-win situation you can think of. Now when you see how big the rewards are, don't you think you can manage just a _few_ extra dollars a month on that house payment?

APPENDIX 8

SOME PROBLEMS OUR READERS HAVE RUN INTO —

HOW WE HELPED THEM

<u>EB of Rockville, MD</u> **wrote to say he was disenchanted with the idea of the Urban Homesteading because he would find it "undesirable" to live in that particular area. Since his income was in the $30's, it was not his style.**

> A call to the District of Columbia Housing Finance Agency (202/628-0311) revealed that they were offering a program for first-time homebuyers at 5% down, 10.75% interest fixed for 30 years, and the income limit to participate in the program was $41,000 for two people in the household.

<u>DT of New York, NY</u> **was feeling discouraged about all the paperwork required to participate in the Urban Development Action Grant program. He is trying to develop 25-40 apartments in a building and have elderly and low income tenants (Section 8).**

> We pointed out that once he had filled out the numerous papers, for future dealings with the government he should only need to recopy essentially the same information. Also, once he had successfully worked with the government on a project, he would know the ropes. He would also have made personal contacts with the many helpful people who act as inspectors and so forth for the government, and it would therefore be much easier for him on future projects.

<u>GP of Compton, CA</u> **wrote to say that only one home per year was available in the Urban Homesteading Program in Compton.**

> The reason the Urban Homesteading Program is not used much out here in California is because the Federal Government puts a limit of $20,000 on the value of the house. Since almost no houses sell for $20,000 or less out here, it is not a practical program. However, there are many other programs which work better for us in California. The City of Los Angeles has developed a Home Mortgage Program. To get the funds to sponser it, the City sells tax-exempt municipal revenue bonds. The funds are then used to allow developers to build new homes or condominiums. At this time (February 1986), they are offered to people meeting certain income levels (for example, to qualify for a 10.39% loan, annual household income may not exceed $38,113; for a 10.45% loan, the household income may not exceed $37,979). The loans are 30-year fixed-rate, and your housing payments ought not to take more than 1/3 of your monthly income. Closing cost are only 1/2%, and the loans are <u>fully assumable</u>. Lastly, the price of the new homes are much

less than comparable homes which were not built under this program.

SP of Madison, OH **was quite upset because it seemed when she called different numbers to ask about the programs, nobody knew what she was talking about. One thing she did find out was that the City Administrator said he was interested in finding out about the programs and setting them up.**

We called the City Administrator, sent him a complimentary copy of our book, together with a book called "Programs of HUD" and SP's name and address so that she and her family might be the first on his list to receive benefits.

There was also a State Financing Agency in Columbus, OH (614/463-9015), and they were coming out with a bond program for which they expected to be offering interest rates of 9-10% with 5% down. The banks working with the program in SP's area were: Central National, National City, Ameritrust, Bank I and Ohio Savings, to name just a few.

SJ of Los Angeles, CA **has a partner, and together they own an 8-unit apartment building which has Section 8 tenants. He sent us a correction on how the Section 8 payments were made, which we have included in this edition, and we talk to him on the phone occasionally to keep up with his progress. At this writing, he was just in the midst of trying to get a low interest loan for another apartment building. Thank you, SJ; we'd like to hear more of your progress.**

The County of Los Angeles (Community Development Commission - 213/725-7407) is offering home improvement loans in certain areas of LA County with amounts up to $27,000 and interest of 3%! The same Community Development Commission (but a different department - 213/725-7418) placed an ad in the Los Angeles Times newspaper saying that they wanted to buy 3-bedroom homes in order to house large low-income families. That could be of interest whether you had a home to sell, or you need a home to live in.

ES of Cleveland, OH **wrote that "I was told by another person that there may not be any more HUD-Approved counseling agencies around ..." and "Have not called finance companies yet, but ... I have recently been in contact with one bank that I'm almost sure (through a neighborhood grapevine) only has about $48,000 in the property, but they insist they are holding out to get $58,000."**

Now, ES is falling victim to the problem which plagues all of us — giving up too soon. She was "told by another person" — she should have called and asked for a HUD-approved counseling agency herself, since there are currently 500+ active and funded in the U.S. at this date. Also, she says she has not actually called the finance companies yet, but goes on to repeat what she has heard "through the neighborhood grapevine" and thus, doesn't herself ever call even one finance company regarding that one property. Now this is exactly what <u>not</u> to do if you hope to have success. You don't take a friend's word for it. You don't even take the clerk's word for it. You <u>know</u> these programs exist, your job is to keep digging and asking until you find out who is doing them in your area. DON'T GIVE UP — THESE PROGRAMS COULD SAVE YOU LITERALLY <u>THOUSANDS</u> OF DOLLARS. YOU COULD BE VERY WELL-PAID FOR ALL YOUR TIME AND EFFORT.

<u>CK of Clifton, NJ</u> **called us, furious, two days after receiving her Homes Book. She was told that there hadn't been any Urban Homesteading in her area since the "early 1970's."**

First of all, the first Urban Homesteading Program wasn't initiated until 1976, so that statement is quite impossible. Next, a call to the closest HUD office to her revealed that they do have an active Urban Homesteading Program there, but only about 3 houses per year are in it. After talking to CK, she said she wouldn't dream of living in an area which was less than desirable, and that her husband earns $35,000 and they have two children.

What the office in her area uses its money for is mostly rehabilitation loans, which they offer at 6%. This is an idea — you can perhaps purchase a home which is very run down, thus paying a very low price, then use the 6% loan to fix it up.

Also, the Clifton Tax Collector's Office (201/473-2661) said they have repossessed houses offered for sale in the fall, and the announcement of them would be published in the legal section of the Herald News for four weeks. There are not a lot of houses which are sold this way, but <u>somebody</u> buys them, and how many houses do you need, anyway?

<u>TR of Minneapolis, MN</u> **wrote to say that he was discouraged because there was a "great deal of competition from a huge group of foreclosure hunters that contact people as soon as the lienholder files in the local county court. My wife ran into no less than 15 other people interested in buying a foreclosure on each morning at the County Recorder's Office for a week. A clerk there told my wife that the foreclosure hunters usually line up before the office even opens in the morning."**

I think that's a good sign! Why do you think those people are so anxious to get to the foreclosure listings? Obviously they think the listings are a good deal. So what if you have to get up early for a week or two? You only need to find one good bargain to live in. Think of how much you could ultimately be saving to wait in that line. Those people wouldn't be there if it wasn't a good deal, so why shouldn't you get in on it, too? Not only that, but foreclosure sales are usually conducted by written bids, so even if there are <u>20</u> other people competing for a property, there's as good a chance that <u>your</u> bid will be chosen as anyone's.

EXAMPLES OF

COMMONLY USED FORMS

INSTRUCTIONS

1. **INVITATION** — Bids are solicited through the public notice of sale. The notice specifies the property to be sold and the time and place of sale. All sales of property are subject to the terms and conditions provided by regulations under section 6335 of the Internal Revenue Code, as stated in the public notice of sale, and as stated in these instructions.

2. **BIDS** — Bids shall be submitted on Internal Revenue Service Form 2222. If the public notice of sale specifies that the property to be sold is offered under alternative methods, such as separately, by groups, and in the aggregate, or by any combination of these methods, bidders may submit bids under one or more of the alternatives. In such cases, a separate Form 2222 shall submitted for each alternative bid, but all bids may be in the same envelope. For the amount of to send with the alternative bids, see instruction No. 4, below.

3. **TIME FOR RECEIVING AND OPENING BIDS** — Bids shall be submitted in a securely sealed envelope. The bidder shall show in the left-hand corner of the envelope his name and and the time and place of sale as announced notice of sale. a bid will to be considered unless it is received by the Internal Revenue Officer conducting the sale prior to the opening of bids. Bids will be opened at the time and place stated in the public notice of sale, or at the time in announcement of the adjournment of the sale.

4. **DEPOSIT WITH BID** — Unless a remittance submitted in accordance with the terms of an agreement to bid on the property now offered for sale, remittance shall be submitted with the bid as follows:

    (a)   If the total bid is $200 or less, the full amount of the bid shall be submitted.

    (b)   If the total bid is more than $200, 20 percent of the bid, or $200, whichever is greater, shall be submitted.

    (c)   If the bidder submits alternative bids for items of property offered separately, by groups, in aggregate, or by any combination of these methods, the bidder shall remit the full amount of the highest alternative bid, if that bid is $200 or less. If the highest alternative bid is more than $200, the bidder shall remit 20 percent of the highest alternative bid, or $200, whichever is greater.

5. **FORM OF REMITTANCE** — All remittances submitted with bids shall be by certified, cashiers', or treasurers' checks drawn on a bank or trust company incorporated under the laws of the United States or under the laws of any State, Territory, or possession of the United States, or by United States postal, bank, express, or telegraph money orders. Remittances shall be made payable to "Internal Revenue Service."

6. **PAYMENT OF BID PRICE** — If the notice of sale states that payment in full is required upon acceptance of the highest bid, payment shall be made at that time. If the notice of sale states that deferred payment is permitted, the balance shall be paid on or before the date fixed for payment thereof. Any remittance submitted with a successful bid will be applied toward the purchase price.

7. **CONDITION OF TITLE AND PROPERTY** — Only the right, title, and interest of the delinquent taxpayer (as identified in the public notice of sale) in and to the property is offered for sale and such interest is offered subject to any prior valid outstanding mortgages, encumbrances, or other liens in favor of third parties against the delinquent taxpayer and which are superior to the lien of the United States. All property is offered for sale "as is" and "where is" and without recourse against the United States. No guaranty or warranty, express or implied, is made as to the validity of the title, quality, quantity, weight, size, or condition of any of the property, or its fitness for any use or purpose. NO claim will be considered for allowance or adjustment or for rescission of the sale based upon failure of the property to conform with any expressed or implied representation.

8. **WITHDRAWAL OF BIDS** — A bid may be withdrawn when a written or telegraphic request is received from the bidder by the Internal Revenue Officer conducting the sale prior to the time fixed for opening the bids. A technical defect in a bid confers no right on the bidder for the withdrawal of his bid after it has been opened. However, the Internal Revenue Officer conducting the sale has the right to waive any technical defects in a bid.

9. **AWARD** — After opening, examining, and considering all bids, the Internal Revenue Officer conducting the sale will announce the amount of the highest bid or, in case of equal bids, the highest bids and the name of the successful bidder(s). If two or more highest bids ar equal in amount, the Internal Revenue Officer conducting the sale will determine the successful bidder by drawing lots. any remittance submitted with an unsuccessful bid will be returned at the end of the sale.

10. **DELIVERY AND REMOVAL OF PERSONAL PROPERTY** — The purchaser assumes the risk of any loss after acceptance of his bid. The United States will retain possession of any personal property until the purchase price has been paid in full. All charges and expenses incurred in for the property after acceptance of the bid shall be borne by the purchase.

11. **REDEMPTION OF PROPERTY AFTER SALE** — If real property is being offered for sale, it will be sold subject to the provisions of Section 6337 of the Internal Revenue Code. The purchaser will be given a certificate of sale as soon as possible after full payment of the purchase price. If the real property is not redeemed the manner and within the time prescribed by Sec 37 the District Director will issue a deed to the p his assigns upon surrender of the certificate of sale.

12. **EFFECT OF JUNIOR ENCUMBRANCES** — A certificate of sale of personal property given, or a deed to real property executed pursuant to Section 6338 shall discharge such property from all liens, encumbrances, and titles over which the lien of the United States with respect to which the levy was made priority.

NOTICE TO PROPERTY IMPROVEMENT LOAN BORROWER(S)

You have applied for a property improvement loan under a program made possible through Title I of the National Housing Act. This program is administered by the U.S. Department of Housing and Urban Development (HUD).

HUD's role in this program is to provide credit insurance to lending institutions making Title I loans. The credit insurance helps you qualify for the loan and protects the lender against major loss if you do not repay the debt.

Although the loan will be obtained through the lending institution, it is a Federal offense for any party to the loan to provide false or misleading information in connection with this loan. Such offense may be punished by a fine, imprisonment or both.

If you do not repay the loan as agreed, the lending institution may declare all unpaid amounts immediately due and payable, with interest, and may then assign the loan to HUD in exchange for Title I insurance benefits. When the loan is assigned to HUD, you will be subject to HUD collection activities, which include (1) Notifying the Internal Revenue Service (the amount due HUD under the assigned note can be treated as income to you if you do not repay it), (2) offsetting against moneys owed to you by Federal agencies, including salary if you are a Federal employee, (3) reporting of the default to credit reporting agencies, (4) possible foreclosure and loss of your home, and (5) referring the defaulted loan to the Department of Justice for legal action.

If you have any questions, please ask your loan officer.

Receipt of a copy of this notice is hereby acknowledged.

DATE: SIGNATURE(S)

_____   _____

_____   _____

PRE-APPLICATION INFORMATION FORM

If you are an FHA Buyer, we will need a copy of the following:

1. Driver's License or picture identification card
2. Social Security Card.
3. Pay Stub — no more than 30 days old.
4. Bank statement(s) — the most recent statement for all bank accounts.

If you are a VA Buyer, we will need the following:

1. Certificate of Eligibility.
2. If you do not have a certificate of Eligibility you will need to bring a copy of your DD-214 or Statement of Service so we can apply for a Certificate of Eligibility.

If you are Self-Employed, we will need the following:

1. The past two years' tax returns.
2. Current Profit and Loss Statement on business and Balance Sheet audited by an accountant.

Don't forget to bring your Sale Contract.

PROPERTY INFORMATION
(Regarding property being financed)

Address_____
_____Zip_____
Name of Condominium or Townhouse, if applicable_____
Lot Size_____ Year Built_____
Legal Description (found on property statement)
_____
_____
_____
_____

Type of Property

Single-family detached	☐	Townhouse	☐
Condominium	☐	Multi-family	☐
Primary Residence	Yes ☐	No ☐	
Has Private Well	Yes ☐	No ☐	
Septic Tank	Yes ☐	No ☐	

Sales Price (not needed if refinance): $_____
Mortgage Amount: $_____

Source of Down Payment and Closing Costs

_____

204

ANSWER ONLY IF YOU'RE REFINANCING

Year Property Acquired_____
Original Cost $_____
Original Mortgage Amount $_____
Cost of Any Improvements $_____
Purpose of Refinancing_____
_____

APPLICANT INFORMATION

Home Phone_____ Business Phone_____
Name_____
Social Security #_____ Age_____
Address (Last Two Years)
Present_____

| | | Own ☐ | |
| Zip_____ | | Rent ☐ | # Years_____ |

Previous_____

| | | Own ☐ | |
| Zip_____ | | Rent ☐ | # Years_____ |

Employment (Last Two Years)
Present_____
Address_____ Zip_____
Telephone (   )_____ Type of Business_____
Contact Person_____ Dept._____
Present Position_____
Starting Date_____
Years in this line of work_____
Gross Monthly Income (Note: enter only income that can be verified in writing)
Monthly base income $_____
Monthly overtime income $_____
Monthly commission income $_____
Monthly dividend & interest income $_____

Previous_____
Address_____ Zip_____
Telephone (   )_____ Type of Business_____
Contact Person_____ Dept._____
Present Position_____
Starting Date_____
Years in this line of work_____
Gross Monthly Income (Note: enter only income that can be verified in writing)
Monthly base income $_____
Monthly overtime income $_____
Monthly commission income $_____

CO-APPLICANT INFORMATION

Home Phone_____ Business Phone_____

Name_____

Social Security #_____ Age_____

Address (Last Two Years)

Present_____

		Own ☐	
_____	Zip_____	Rent ☐	# Years_____

Previous_____

		Own ☐	
_____	Zip_____	Rent ☐	# Years_____

Employment (Last Two Years)

Present_____

Address_____ Zip_____

Telephone (   )_____   Type of Business_____

Contact Person_____   Dept._____

Present Position_____

Starting Date_____

Years in this line of work_____

Gross Monthly Income (Note: enter only income that can be verified in writing)

Monthly base income $_____

Monthly overtime income $_____

Monthly commission income $_____

Monthly dividend & interest income $_____

Previous_____

Address_____ Zip_____

Telephone (   )_____   Type of Business_____

Contact Person_____   Dept._____

Present Position_____

Starting Date_____

Years in this line of work_____

Gross Monthly Income (Note: enter only income that can be verified in writing)

Monthly base income $_____

Monthly overtime income $_____

Monthly commission income $_____

OTHER INCOME

Source_____   Monthly Amount $_____

Source_____   Monthly Amount $_____

(Bring supporting document such as leases, divorce decrees, W-2's, etc.)

206

BANK ACCOUNTS
(Include credit unions, S&L's, etc.; and also any money market or CD amounts)

1.   Bank Name_____
       Address_____ Zip_____
       Checking   Savings
       Account #_____   Account #_____
       Checking   Savings
       Balance $_____   Balance $_____

2.   Bank Name_____
       Address_____ Zip_____
       Checking   Savings
       Account #_____   Account #_____
       Checking   Savings
       Balance $_____   Balance $_____

3.   Bank Name_____
       Address_____ Zip_____
       Checking   Savings
       Account #_____   Account #_____
       Checking   Savings
       Balance $_____   Balance $_____

STOCKS, BONDS, OR OTHER SECURITIES
Please attach a list showing:

Name of Stock_____
Amount per share $_____
Number of shares_____
Or you may wish to bring a current brokerage statement.

VEHICLES
Including Autos, Trucks, Campers, Boats, Trailers, etc.

Year & Make_____   Value $_____
Year & Make_____   Value $_____
Year & Make_____   Value $_____
Year & Make_____   Value $_____

VALUE OF FURNITURE & PERSONAL BELONGINGS
$ _____

LIABILITIES (CREDITORS)

List all charge accounts, credit cards, bank loans, and installment debt, etc., if there is a current balance due. Do not list first or second mortgages here.

1. Firm Name_____
    Address_____
    Account #_____
    Balance Owed $_____
    Monthly Payment $_____

2. Firm Name_____
    Address_____
    Account #_____
    Balance Owed $_____
    Monthly Payment $_____

3. Firm Name_____
    Address_____
    Account #_____
    Balance Owed $_____
    Monthly Payment $_____

4. Firm Name_____
    Address_____
    Account #_____
    Balance Owed $_____
    Monthly Payment $_____

5. Firm Name_____
    Address_____
    Account #_____
    Balance Owed $_____
    Monthly Payment $_____

6. Firm Name_____
    Address_____
    Account #_____
    Balance Owed $_____
    Monthly Payment $_____

MONTHLY RENT OR MORTGAGE PAYMENT
(Last Two Years)

Present:
Landlord or Lender_____
Address_____ Zip_____
Loan/Apt. #_____ FHA ❑   Conv. ❑   VA ❑
Balance Owed $_____ Monthly Payment $_____
Equity $_____

208

Previous
Landlord or Lender_____
Address_____ Zip_____
Loan/Apt. #_____

OTHER HOUSING EXPENSES
(Report separately items 1, 2, 3 only if they are not included in your monthly mortgage payment)

1.   Homeowners insurance_____
2.   Real Estate Tax_____
3.   Mortgage insurance, if applicable_____
4.   Monthly utility expenses (i.e. heat, light, water)_____
      Other mortgage payment, if you currently have a
second mortgage_____

OTHER REAL ESTATE OWNED
Please attach a list showing the following information for all other real estate currently owned.

Lender_____
Address_____ Zip_____
Loan/Apt. #_____ FHA ☐ Conv. ☐ VA ☐
Balance Owed $_____ Monthly Payment $_____
Equity $_____

| Title I Refinanced Loan(s)
 ☐ Yes ☐ No | HUD/FHA Title I Loan(s) | Balance Owing |

Notice: If this structure was built before 1950, it may contain lead-based paint which, if eaten, may cause mental retardation, blindness, paralysis, or even death. Symptoms may include stomach aches, vomiting, headaches, a loss of appetite, crankiness or frequent tiredness. A child who has any of these symptoms or who is suspected of having eaten lead-based paint should be taken immediately to your local doctor, clinic or hospital for screening or treatment. The best way to prevent lead-based paint poisoning is to keep you home in good shape and to assure the removal of immediate lead-based paint hazards. Once the hazards have been removed, the walls should then be repainted with two coats of unleaded paint. For detailed information on the prevention and elimination of lead-based paint hazards, please contact your local HUD office for a free pamphlet entitled "Lead Poisoning: Watch Out for Lead-Base Paint."

Description of Improvement	Name and Address of Contractor/Dealer
Estimated Cost	
Description of Improvement	Name and Address of Contractor/Dealer
Estimated Cost	
Description of Improvement	Name and Address of Contractor/Dealer
Estimated Cost	
Description of Improvement	Name and Address of Contractor/Dealer
Estimated Cost	

Warning: Any person who knowingly makes a false statement or misrepresentation in this application or causes such a false statement or misrepresentation to be made be subject to a fine of not more than $5000 or by imprisonment for not more than two years, under provisions of the United States Criminal Code.

Important — Applicant Read Before Signing

The selection of a Contractor or Dealer, acceptance of materials used, and work performed is your responsibility. The HUD/FHA does not guarantee the material or workmanship or inspects the work performed. I (We) certify that the above statements are true, accurate, and complete to the best of my (our) knowledge and belief. This application shall remain the property of the Lending Institution to which submitted purpose of obtaining a loan. I (We) hereby consent to and authorize the Lending Institution of the HUD/FHA giving the reasonable notice, to enter the improved property for the purpose of determining that the improvements specified in this application have been completed.

| Name (Applicant) | (LS) | Name (Co-Applicant) | (LS) |

Note to Salesperson: If proceeds will be disbursed to the Contractor/Dealer, the person(s) selling the above described improvements must sign the following certification:

I (We) certify that: 1) I (We) am (are) the person(s) who sold the job; 2) The Contract contains the whole agreement with the borrower; 3) The borrower has not been given or promised a cash payment or rebate nor has it been represented to the borrower that he or she will receive a cash bonus or commission on future sales as an inducement for the consummation of this transaction; that the improvements have not been misrepresented; no promise impossible of attainment; no encouragement of trial purchase; no promise that the improvements will be used as a model for advertising or other demonstration purposes; and no offer of debt consolidation.

| Name | (LS) |
| | (My true name and signature are as shown above) |

If application is prepared by one other than the applicant, the person preparing the application must sign below. I (We) certify that the statements made herein are based upon information given to me (us) by the borrower(s) and are accurate to the best of my (our) knowledge and belief.

| Prepared By: | Name and Address of Contractor/Dealer |
| Representing: | |

(Reserved for use of Lending Institution)

FORM 2435 (Rev. Jan. 1970)	DEPARTMENT OF THE TREASURY - INTERNAL REVENUE SERVICE ## Certificate of Sale of Seized Property

I hereby certify that I sold at public sale the property described below seized for nonpayment of delinquent Internal Revenue taxes due from:

Taxpayer:_____

Date of Sale:_____ Sale Held At:_____

_____ In the Country Of _____

Description Of Property Sold:

(if space is needed, please continue on back)

The above property was sold ate the highest bid received of which the receipt is hereby acknowledged.

Sale Amount $_____ Purchaser_____

Purchaser's Address_____

The sale was conducted in accordance with the provisions of Subchapter D, Chapter 64 of the Internal Revenue Code and the regulations thereunder.

PERSONAL PROPERTY

This certificate transfers to the purchaser named above all right, title and interest of the taxpayer shown in and to the personal property described.

REAL PROPERTY

If the real property described above it not redeemed within the time prescribed in Section 6337 of the Internal Revenue code, a quitclaim deed will be issued upon surrender of this certificate. The deed will operate as a conveyance of the right, title, and interest of the taxpayer shown above in and to the real property described. Instructions for surrender of this certificate and redemption provisions are on the back of this document.

REVENUE OFFICER *(Signature)*	DISTRICT
REVENUE OFFICER'S ADDRESS	DATE

FORM 2435 (REV. 1070)

Credit Application for Property Improvement Loan

Please Answer All Questions

U.S. Department of Housing and Urban Development
Office of Housing
Federal Housing Commissioner

OMB Approval No. 2502-0328 (Exp. 7-31-89)

This application is submitted to obtain credit under the provisions of Title I of the National Housing Act. **Please Answer All Questions**

Privacy Act Notice – The information requested in this form is to be used by the Department of Housing and Urban Development (HUD) in the accounting of Title I loans and in the monitoring of Title I funds. It will not be disclosed or released outside of HUD and the Lending Institution which will provide the funds except as required and permitted by law. You do not have to give us this information, but, if you do not provide the information necessary to an evaluation of credit worthiness your application may be delayed or rejected. The Department of HUD is authorized to ask for this information by Title I, Section 2 of the National Housing Act (48 Stat., 1246, 12 U.S.C. 1701 et seq.).

General Information – Applicants are required to provide their social security number. However, the answers to questions relating to marital status, race and sex are voluntary and are requested solely for the purpose of determining compliance with Federal Civil Rights law and your response will not affect consideration of your application. By providing this information, you will assist us in assuring that this program is administered in a nondiscriminatory manner. If you feel you have been discriminated against and you want to report it, the Fair Housing and Equal Opportunity Hotline Number is 800-424-8590.

I/We hereby apply for a loan of $ _____ (net) to repaid in _____ months. Date _____

1. Do you have any past due obligations owned or insured by any agency of the Federal Government? (If the answer is "Yes" you are not eligible to apply for an FHA Title I loan until the existing debt has been brought current.) Check appropriate box ☐ Yes ☐ No

2. Have you any other application for an FHA Title I Loan pending at this time? If "Yes" with whom — Name and Address   ☐ Yes ☐ No

3. Are there any unsatisfied judgements against you?   ☐ Yes ☐ No

Have you been declared bankrupt in the last seven years?   ☐ Yes ☐ No

Explain any "Yes" answers

3. Applicant(s)

Name of Applicant	Name of Co-Applicant (if any)
Social Security Number / Telephone Number	Social Security Number / Telephone Number
Present Address	Present Address
How Long?	How Long?
Previous Address	Previous Address
How Long?	How Long?

Marital Status
☐ Married ☐ Separated ☐ Unmarried (Including Single, Divorced, Widowed)

Marital Status
☐ Married ☐ Separated ☐ Unmarried (Including Single, Divorced, Widowed)

| Sex ☐ Male ☐ Female | Date of Birth | Number of Dependents | Sex ☐ Male ☐ Female | Date of Birth | Number of Dependents |

Check Appropriate Box
1. ☐ White 2. ☐ Black 3. ☐ American Indian or Alaskan Native
4. ☐ Asian or Pacific Islander 5. ☐ Hispanic

Check Appropriate Box
1. ☐ White 2. ☐ Black 3. ☐ American Indian or Alaskan Native
4. ☐ Asian or Pacific Islander 5. ☐ Hispanic

Name and Address of Nearest Relative Not Living With You	Name and Address of Nearest Relative Not Living With You
Relationship / Telephone Number	Relationship / Telephone Number

4. Employment and Salaries (If applicant is self-employed, submit current financial statement.)

Applicant's Employer Name and Business Address	Co-applicant's Employer Name and Business Address
Business Phone / Type of Work or Position	Business Phone / Type of Work or Position

Replaces HUD-56001(8-84) which may be used until supply is exhausted

HUD-56001 (8-8
(HB 4700.

Number of Years	Salary per week or month	Number of Years	Salary per week or month
	$ per		$ per

Applicant's Previous Employer's Name and Business Address	Co-applicant's Previous Employer's Name and Business Address

Business Phone	Type of Work or Position	Business Phone	Type of Work or Position

Number of years	Salary per week or month (Gross)	Number of years	Salary per week or month (Gross)
	$ per		$ per

Other Income Source (Note: Income from alimony, child support, or separate maintenance income need not be reported unless you will rely upon it as a basis for undertaking or repaying this loan.)

Applicant(s) Source	Amount per week or month	Co-Applicant(s) Source	Amount per week or month
	$ per		$ per

5. Bank Account

Applicant(s)			Co-Applicant(s)		
☐ Yes ☐ No	☐ Checking	☐ Savings	☐ Yes ☐ No	☐ Checking	☐ Savings

Name and Address of Bank or Branch	Name and Address of Bank or Branch

6. Debts - List all fixed obligations, installment accounts, FHA loans, and debts to banks, finance companies and Government agencies.
(If more space is needed, list all additional debts on separate pages and attach them to this form.)

Automotive Liens		Present Balance	Monthly Payment	Amount Past Due
Lein Holder	Year and Make	$	$	$
Lein Holder	Year and Make	$	$	$

To Whom Indebted (Name)	Account No.	City and State	FHA Insured Yes	No	Date Incurred	Original Amount	Present Balance	Monthly Payment	Amount Past Due
						$	$	$	$
						$	$	$	$
						$	$	$	$
						$	$	$	$
						$	$	$	$

7. Property to be Improved

Is this a new residential structure? ☐ Yes ☐ No	If yes, has it been completed and occupied for 90 days or longer? ☐ Yes ☐ No

Address (Number, Street, City, State and Zip Code)	Type - Home, Apt., Store, Farm, etc., (If Apt., Number of Units):

Fill in One

Is Owned By	Is Leased By

Payments Made To	Payments Made To

Being Brought On (Check One) ☐ Contract ☐ Mortgage ☐ Deed or Trust

Purchase Price	Balance Owing	Monthly Payment	Lease Expiration

Year Built	Date of Purchase	Year Built	

Completion Certificate for Property Improvements

Direct or Dealer Loan

U.S. Department of Housing
and Urban Development

Office of Housing
Federal Housing Commissioner

OMB Approval No. 2502-0328 (Exp. 7-31-89)

Name and Address of Lending Institution	Names and Addresses of Borrowers

Address of Improved Property

Check One

☐ Direct Loan   ☐ Dealer Loan

Notice to Borrowers: You must execute this certificate as a condition of loan approval. Do Not Sign this certificate until the dealer or contractor has satisfactorily completed the improvements in accordance with the terms of your contract or sales agreement.

I(we) certify that:

(1) The loan proceeds have been spent on property improvements that are eligible under the Title I regulations and in accordance with the contract or cost estimate furnished to the lender with my(our) credit application.

(2) The property improvements have been completed in general accordance with the contract or cost estimate and to my(our) satisfaction.

(3) I(we) have not obtained and will not receive any cash payment, rebate, cash bonus, sales commission, or anything of value in excess of $10 from the dealer or contractor as an inducement to enter into this loan transaction.

(4) I(we) understand that the selection of the dealer or contractor and the acceptance of the materials used and the work performed is my(our) responsibility, and HUD does not guarantee the quality or workmanship of the property improvements.

Signature of Borrower (Read before signing)	Date Signed	Signature of Borrower (Read before signing)	Date Signed

Notice to Dealer or Contractor: You must execute this certificate for all dealer-originated loans, and for all direct loans where you are responsible for supplying materials and carrying out improvement work under a written contract or sales agreement. If any of the following representations prove incorrect, you may be required to promptly repurchase the loan from the lending institution or from HUD, as the case may be.

The undersigned certifies that:

(1) The property improvements are eligible under the Title I regulations and in accordance with the contract or cost estimate furnished to the borrowers.

(2) The property improvements have been completed in general accordance with the contract or cost estimate and to the satisfaction of the borrowers.

(3) The borrowers have not been given or promised any cash payment, rebate, cash bonus, sales commission, or anything of value in excess of $10 as an inducement to enter into this loan transaction (except for any discount points paid by the undersigned to the lender).

(4) The borrowers signed this certificate after completion of the property improvements, and all signatures on this certificate are genuine.

Name and Address of Dealer or Contractor	Signature and Title	Date
Name and Address of Dealer or Contractor	Signature and Title	Date
Name and Address of Dealer or Contractor	Signature and Title	Date

Warning: Any person who knowingly makes a false statement or a misrepresentation in this certificate shall be subject to a fine of not more than $5,000 or to imprisonment for not more than 2 years, or both, under provisions of the United States Criminal Code.

Previous Edition Obsolete

1. Lender Copy

HUD-56002 (6-87)
HB4700.

VETERANS ADMINISTRATION, U.S. DEPARTMENT OF AGRICULTURE (Farmers Home Administration) and U.S. DEPARTMENT OF HOUSING AND URBAN DEVELOPMENT (Community Planning and Development, and Housing - Federal Housing Commissioner)

REQUEST FOR VERIFICATION OF EMPLOYMENT

PRIVACY ACT NOTICE: This information is to be used by the agency collecting it in determining whether you qualify as a prospective mortgagor or borrower under its program. It will not be disclosed outside the agency without your consent except to your employer(s) for verification of employment and as required and permitted by law. You do not have to give us this information, but if you do not, your application for approval as a prospective mortgagor or borrower may be delayed or rejected. The information requested in this form is authorized by Title 38, U.S.C., Chapter 37 (if VA); by 12 U.S.C., Section 1701 et seq. (if HUD/FHA); by 42 U.S.C., Section 1425b (if HUD/CPD); and by 42 U.S.C., Section 1471 et seq., or 7 U.S.C. Section 1921 et seq. (if U.S.D.A., FmHA).

INSTRUCTIONS – LENDER OR LPA (LOCAL PROCESSING AGENCY): Complete Items 1 through 7. Have the applicant complete Item 8. Forward the completed form directly to the employer named in Item 1. EMPLOYER: Complete either Parts II and IV or Parts III and IV. Return the form directly to the lender or local processing agency named in Item 2 of Part I.

PART I. REQUEST

1. TO: *(Name and address of employer)*	2. FROM: *(Name and address of lender or local processing agency)*

I certify that this verification has been sent directly to the employer and has not passed through the hands of the applicant or any other interested party.

4. TITLE OF LENDER, OFFICIAL OF LPA, OR FmHA LOAN PACKAGER	
5. DATE	6. HUD/FHA/CPD, VA, OR FmHA NO.

3. SIGNATURE OF LENDER, OFFICIAL OF LPA, OR FmHA LOAN PACKAGER

I have applied for a mortgage/rehabilitation loan and stated that I am/was employed by you. My signature below authorizes verification of my employment information.

7. NAME AND ADDRESS OF APPLICANT

8. EMPLOYEE'S IDENTIFICATION

SIGNATURE OF APPLICANT

PART II. VERIFICATION OF PRESENT EMPLOYMENT

EMPLOYMENT DATA	PAY DATA

9. APPLICANT'S EMPLOYMENT DATE

12A. BASE PAY (Current)

$ _____ ANNUAL	$ _____ HOURLY
$ _____ MONTHLY	$ _____ WEEKLY
$ _____ OTHER *(Specify)*	

10. PRESENT POSITION

FOR MILITARY PERSONNEL ONLY

TYPE *(Taxable Pay)*	MTHLY. AMT.
BASE PAY	$
PRO PAY	$
FLIGHT PAY	$

11. PROBABILITY OF CONTINUED EMPLOYMENT

CAREER SEA PAY	$
OTHER *(Specify)*	$

12B. EARNINGS

13. IF OVERTIME OR BONUS IS APPLICABLE, IS IT LIKELY TO CONTINUE?

TYPE	YR. TO DATE	PAST YR.	TYPE *(Nontaxable Pay)*	MTHLY. AMT.
BASE PAY	$	$	QUARTERS	$
OVERTIME	$	$	RATIONS *(Subsistence)*	$
COMMISSIONS	$	$	CLOTHING	$
BONUS	$	$	VHA	$

OVERTIME ☐ YES ☐ NO
BONUS ☐ YES ☐ NO

14. IF PAID HOURLY, INDICATE AVERAGE WEEKLY HOURS WORKED DURING CURRENT AND PAST YEAR

OTHER *(Specify)*	$

PART III. VERIFICATION OF PREVIOUS EMPLOYMENT

15. DATES OF EMPLOYMENT

16. SALARY/WAGE AT TERMINATION PER ☐ YEAR ☐ MONTH ☐ WEEK

BASE PAY	OVERTIME	COMMISSIONS	BONUS
$	$	$	$

17. POSITION HELD

18. REASON(S) FOR LEAVING

PART IV. CERTIFICATION

Federal statutes provide severe penalties for any fraud, intentional misrepresentation, or criminal connivance or conspiracy purposed to influence the issuance of any guaranty or insurance by the VA Administrator, a U.S.D.A., FmHA Administrator, the HUD/FHA Commissioner, or the HUD/CPD Assistant Secretary.

19. SIGNATURE	20. TITLE OF EMPLOYER	21. DATE

Previous Editions May Be Used Until Supply Is Exhausted.

HUD-82J3/92004-g, VA 26-8497, FmHA-410-5

RETURN DIRECTLY TO LENDER OR LOCAL PROCESSING AGENCY

FORM 2222
(REV. OCT. 1969)

SEALED BID FOR PURCHASE OF SEIZED PROPERTY

(Pursuant to Section 6335 of the Internal Revenue Code)

Terms and conditions of sealed bid sales are provided in regulations under section 6335 of the Internal Revenue Code and are summarized in the instructions on the back of this form. TO FILL OUT THIS FORM, PLEASE TYPE OR PRINT PLAINLY, EXCEPT FOR SIGNATURES.

NAME AND ADDRESS OF BIDDER	BID MADE BY: *(Check appropriate box)*
	☐ INDIVIDUAL ☐ PARTNERSHIP ☐ CORP.

ITEM OR GROUP NO.	DESCRIPTION OF PROPERTY (Description must conform to that in the public notice of sale without qualification or reservation. Attach separate sheets if necessary.)	AMOUNT BID
	TOTAL AMOUNT OF BID	$

Remittance enclosed in the amount of _____ dollars.

$_____ *(See instruction 4 and 5. If remittance has been submitted with alternative bid, so state.)*

SIGNATURE OF AUTHORIZED PERSON	NAME AND TITLE *(Type or Print)*	DATE

(THIS SPACE RESERVED FOR USE OF DISTRICT DIRECTOR)

AWARD		RETURN OF REMITTANCE TO UNSUCCESSFUL BIDDER
ACCEPTED AS TO ITEMS OR GROUPS NUMBERED		I hereby acknowledge receipt of remittance submitted with his bid.
TOTAL AMOUNT OF ACCEPTED BID	$	
REMITTANCE APPLIED TO BID		
BALANCE DUE ON *(Date)*	$	SIGNATURE, TITLE AND DATE
SIGNATURE AND TITLE		
		REMITTANCE RETURNED BY MAIL ON *(Date)*
ADDRESS		
		SIGNATURE OF REVENUE OFFICER
CERTIFICATE OF SALE ISSUED ON *(Date)*		

FORM 2222 (REV. 10-1)

Residential Loan Application

MORTGAGE APPLIED FOR	☐ Conventional ☐ FHA ☑ VA ☐	Amount $	Interest Rate %	No. of Months	Monthly Payment Principal & Interest $	Escrow/Impounds (to be collected monthly) ☐ Taxes ☐ Hazard Ins. ☐ Mtg. Ins. ☐ ____
Prepayment Option						

Subject Property

Property Street Address	City	County	State	Zip	No. Units

Legal Description (Attach description if necessary) — Year Built

Purpose of Loan: ☐ Purchase ☐ Construction-Permanent ☐ Construction ☐ Refinance ☐ Other (Explain)

Complete this line if Construction-Permanent or Construction Loan ☛	Lot Value Data Year Acquired $	Original Cost $	Present Value (a) $	Cost of Imps. (b) $	Total (a + b)	ENTER TOTAL AS PURCHASE PRICE IN DETAILS OF PURCHASE ☛

Complete this line if a Refinance Loan	Purpose of Refinance	Describe Improvements [ ] made [ ] to be made
Year Acquired Original Cost $ Amt. Existing Liens $		Cost: $

Title Will Be Held In What Name(s) — Manner In Which Title Will Be Held

Source of Down Payment and Settlement Charges

This application is designed to be completed by the borrower(s) with the lender's assistance. The Co-Borrower Section and all other Co-Borrower questions must be completed and the appropriate box(es) checked if ☐ another person will be jointly obligated with the Borrower on the loan, or ☐ the Borrower is relying on income from alimony, child support or separate maintenance or on the income or assets of another person as a basis for repayment of the loan, or ☐ the Borrower is married and resides, or the property is located, in a community property state.

Borrower			Co-Borrower		
Name	Age	School Yrs	Name	Age	School Yrs
Present Address No. Years ____ ☐ Own ☐ Rent			Present Address No. Years ____ ☐ Own ☐ Rent		
Street			Street		
City/State/Zip			City/State/Zip		
Former address if less than 2 years at present address			Former address if less than 2 years at present address		
Street			Street		
City/State/Zip			City/State/Zip		
Years at former address ☐ Own ☐ Rent			Years at former address ☐ Own ☐ Rent		
Marital Status ☐ Married ☐ Separated ☐ Unmarried (incl. single, divorced, widowed) DEPENDENTS OTHER THAN LISTED BY CO BORROWER NO. AGES			Marital Status ☐ Married ☐ Separated ☐ Unmarried (incl. single, divorced, widowed) DEPENDENTS OTHER THAN LISTED BY BORROWER NO. AGES		
Name and Address of Employer	Years employed in this line of work or profession? ____ years Years on this job ____ ☐ Self Employed*		Name and Address of Employer	Years employed in this line of work or profession? ____ years Years on this job ____ ☐ Self Employed*	
Position/Title	Type of Business		Position/Title	Type of Business	
Social Security Number ***	Home Phone	Business Phone	Social Security Number ***	Home Phone	Business Phone

Gross Monthly Income				Monthly Housing Expense**			Details of Purchase	
Item	Borrower	Co-Borrower	Total	Rent	PRESENT $	PROPOSED	Do Not Complete If Refinance	
Base Empl. Income	$	$	$	First Mortgage (P&I)		$	a. Purchase Price	$
Overtime				Other Financing (P&I)			b. Total Closing Costs (Est.)	
Bonuses				Hazard Insurance			c. Prepaid Escrows (Est.)	
Commissions				Real Estate Taxes			d. Total (a + b + c)	$
Dividends/Interest				Mortgage Insurance			e. Amount This Mortgage	( )
Net Rental Income				Homeowner Assn. Dues			f. Other Financing	( )
Other† (Before completing, see notice under Describe Other Income below.)				Other:			g. Other Equity	( )
				Total Monthly Pmt.	$	$	Amount of Cash Deposit	( )
				Utilities			Closing Costs Paid by Seller	( )
Total	$	$	$	Total	$	$	Cash Reqd. For Closing (Est.)	$

Describe Other Income

NOTICE: † Alimony, child support, or separate maintenance income need not be revealed if the Borrower or Co-Borrower does not choose to have it considered as a basis for repaying this loan.

◁ B—Borrower C—Co-Borrower	Monthly Amount

If Employed In Current Position For Less Than Two Years, Complete the Following

B/C	Previous Employer/School	City/State	Type of Business	Position/Title	Dates From/To	Monthly Income
						$

If a "yes" answer is given to a question in this column, please explain on an attached sheet.	Borrower Yes or No	Co-Borrower Yes or No
Are there any outstanding judgments against you?		
Have you been declared bankrupt within the past 7 years?		
Have you had property foreclosed upon or given title or deed in lieu thereof in the last 7 years?		
Are you a party to a law suit?		
Are you obligated to pay alimony, child support, or separate maintenance?		
Is any part of the down payment borrowed?		
Are you a co-maker or endorser on a note?		

	Borrower Yes or No	Co-Borrower Yes or No
Are you a U.S. citizen?		
If "no," are you a resident alien?		
If "no," are you a non-resident alien?		
Explain Other Financing or Other Equity (if any).		

*FHLMC/FNMA require business credit report, signed Federal Income Tax returns for last two years; and, if available, audited Profit and Loss Statement plus balance sheet for same period.
**All Present Monthly Housing Expenses of Borrower and Co-Borrower should be listed on a combined basis.
***Optional for FHLMC
FHLMC 65 Rev. 10/86   ! Maynard Printing, Inc. • 219 New York Avenue • Des Moines, Iowa 50313

Fannie Mae Form 1003 Rev. 10/86

This Statement and any applicable supporting schedules may be completed jointly by both married and unmarried co-borrowers if their assets and liabilities are sufficiently joined so that the Statement can be meaningfully and fairly presented on a combined basis; otherwise separate Statements and Schedules are required (FHLMC 65A/FNMA 1003A). If the co-borrower section was completed about a spouse, this statement and supporting schedules must be completed about that spouse also. ☐ Completed Jointly ☐ Not Completed Jointly

Assets | Liabilities and Pledged Assets

Indicate by (*) those liabilities or pledged assets which will be satisfied upon sale of real estate owned or upon refinancing of subject property.

Description	Cash or Market Value	Creditors' Name, Address and Account Number		Acct. Name if Not Borrower's	Mo. Pmt. and Mos. Left to Pay	Unpaid Balance
Cash Deposit Toward Purchase Held By	$	Installment Debts (Include "revolving" charge accounts)			$ Pmt/Mos.	$
		Co.	Acct. No.			
Checking and Savings Accounts (Show Names of Institutions (Account Numbers) Bank, S & L or Credit Union		Addr.				
		City			/	
Addr.		Co.	Acct. No.			
		Addr.				
City		City			/	
Acct. No.		Co.	Acct. No.			
Bank, S & L or Credit Union		Addr.				
		City			/	
Addr.		Co.	Acct. No.			
City		Addr.				
Acct. No.		City			/	
Bank, S & L or Credit Union		Co.	Acct. No.			
		Addr.				
Addr.		City			/	
City		Other Debts including Stock Pledges				
Acct. No.					/	
Stocks and Bonds (No./Description)						
		Real Estate Loans Co.	Acct. No.		✕	
		Addr.				
		City				
Life Insurance Net Cash Value Face Amount $		Co.	Acct. No		✕	
		Addr.				
Subtotal Liquid Assets		City				
Real Estate Owned (Enter Market Value from Schedule of Real Estate Owned)		Automobile Loans Co.	Acct. No.			
Vested Interest in Retirement Fund		Addr.				
Net worth of Business Owned (ATTACH FINANCIAL STATEMENT)		City			/	
		Co.	Acct. No.			
Automobiles Owned (Make and Year)		City				
Furniture and Personal Property		Alimony/Child Support/Separate Maintenance Payments Owed to				✕
Other Assets (Itemize)						
		Total Monthly Payments			$	
Total Assets	A $	Net Worth (A minus B) $			Total Liabilities	B $

SCHEDULE OF REAL ESTATE OWNED (If Additional Properties Owned Attach Separate Schedule)

Address of Property (Indicate S if Sold, PS if Pending Sale or R if Rental being held for income)		Type of Property	Present Market Value	Amount of Mortgages & Liens	Gross Rental Income	Mortgage Payments	Taxes, Ins. Maintenance and Misc.	Net Rental Income
			$	$	$	$	$	$
		TOTALS →	$	$	$	$	$	$

List Previous Credit References

B–Borrower C–Co-Borrower	Creditor's Name and Address	Account Number	Purpose	Highest Balance	Date Paid
				$	

List any additional names under which credit has previously been received _____

AGREEMENT: The undersigned applies for the loan indicated in this application to be secured by a first mortgage or deed of trust on the property described herein, and represents that the property will not be used for any illegal or restricted purpose, and that all statements made in this application are true and are made for the purpose of obtaining the loan. Verification may be obtained from any source named in this application. The original or a copy of this application will be retained by the lender, even if the loan is not granted. The undersigned ☐ intend or ☐ do not intend to occupy the property as their primary residence.

I/we fully understand that it is a federal crime punishable by fine or imprisonment, or both, to knowingly make any false statements concerning any of the above facts as applicable under the provisions of Title 18, United States Code, Section 1014.

_____ Date _____ _____ Date _____
Borrower's Signature Co-Borrower's Signature

Information for Government Monitoring Purposes

The following information is requested by the Federal Government for certain types of loans related to a dwelling, in order to monitor the lender's compliance with equal credit opportunity and fair housing laws. You are not required to furnish this information, but are encouraged to do so. The law provides that a lender may neither discriminate on the basis of this information, nor on whether you choose to furnish it. However, if you choose not to furnish it, under Federal regulations this lender is required to note race and sex on the basis of visual observation or surname. If you do not wish to furnish the above information, please check the box below. (Lender must review the above material to assure that the disclosures satisfy all requirements to which the Lender is subject under applicable state law for the particular type of loan applied for.)

Borrower: ☐ I do not wish to furnish this information
Race/National Origin:
☐ American Indian, Alaskan Native ☐ Asian, Pacific Islander
☐ Black ☐ Hispanic ☐ White
☐ Other (specify): _____
Sex: ☐ Female ☐ Male

Co-Borrower: ☐ I do not wish to furnish this information
Race/National Origin:
☐ American Indian, Alaskan Native ☐ Asian, Pacific Islander
☐ Black ☐ Hispanic ☐ White
☐ Other (specify): _____
Sex: ☐ Female ☐ Male

To Be Completed by Interviewer

This application was taken by:
☐ face to face interview
☐ by mail
☐ by telephone

_____
Interviewer

_____
Name of Interviewer's Employer

_____
Interviewer's Phone Number

_____
Address of Interviewer's Employer

FHLMC Form 65 Rev. 10/86   REVERSE   Fannie Mae Form 1003 Rev. 10/86